Retriever Trouble- shooting

Retriever Trouble- shooting

Strategies & Solutions to Retriever Training Problems

JOHN AND AMY DAHL

WILLOW CREEK PRESS
Minocqua, Wisconsin

Published by Willow Creek Press
P.O. Box 147, Minocqua, Wisconsin 54548
For information on other Willow Creek Press titles, call 1-800-850-9453

Editor: Andrea Donner

Photo Credits:
Jami Lupold: p.10, 14, 20, 22, 27, 50, 51, 56, 62, 66, 67, 69, 70, 74, 76, 78, 87, 90, 93, 105, 109, 115, 125, 130, 139, 150, 158, 159, 162, 165, 198, 208, 228, 229, 232, 233

Brendan Sullivan: p.154, 172, 177, 211, 217, 218

John & Amy Dahl: p.16, 25, 36, 38, 40, 52, 53, 81, 86, 95, 100, 106, 128, 141, 152, 184, 185, 191, 193, 203

R. Tamara de Silva: p.223

Library of Congress Cataloging-in-Publication Data

Dahl, John I.
  Retriever troubleshooting : retriever training methods and solutions to training problems / John and Amy Dahl.
      p. cm.
  ISBN 1-57223-783-X (softcover : alk. paper)
  1. Retrievers--Training. 2. Hunting dogs--Training. I. Dahl, Amy, 1962-
II. Title.
  SF429.R4D345 2006
  636.752'735--dc22
                              2006001045

Printed in United States of America

DEDICATION

To Ruth Ariadne Dahl and Charles Joseph Dahl

ACKNOWLEDGEMENTS

We wish to thank those individuals who have helped out when called upon. We are especially indebted to Richard Frost and Anne Stewart Frost, and, in the retriever community, to Mike Osteen and Jennifer Wallace. Others have been there when needed, and we are grateful.

We thank Jami Lupold and Brendan Sullivan for their photography. We thank Ry and Sally Tipton, Joseph and Janice Smith, Terry and Sheri O'Brien, Jami Lupold, Don Eason, and Tamara de Silva for allowing us to use pictures of their dogs. We thank Jennifer Wallace for allowing us to include pictures of her puppies, her daughter, and herself.

We are grateful to the readers of our first book who encouraged us to write this one. Finally we thank Andrea Donner and Willow Creek Press for their commitment and patience.

John and Amy Dahl

TABLE OF CONTENTS

INTRODUCTION

ALMOST ALL RETRIEVERS, during the course of their working lives, undergo setbacks, snags, and difficulties of one sort or another. Ideally, thorough and proper early preparation should set the stage for a life of steady progress based on a sound foundation. Ideals, however, are rarely realized. No matter how careful our early training efforts, holes are going to appear.

The fact that every dog is unique suggests that absolutist training programs are unlikely to yield consistent results. We train as though there is substantial similarity among retrievers, but we also vary our methods, including the order and amount of time applied to all phases of training.

Good training requires identification of incipient problems before they reach the point at which they are difficult to rectify. Violations such as creeping, barking, fighting, and rough mouthing birds are hard to correct once they become habitual.

Other faults such as switching, poor hunt, lining failures, bugging, poor whistle stopping, and handling refusals, can develop gradually, and are usually a result of inadequate attention to these shortcomings during daily training. Take note when a friend you have not seen for some time says, "Blackie

What we want: clean, enthusaistic, direct retrieves.

doesn't seem to line as well as he used to." The change might have been so gradual that you didn't notice it.

Often, all that is required when backsliding and development of bad habits occurs, is to readjust your training so as to even things out. Sometimes more is needed.

Training, particularly at the advanced levels, is a creative endeavor. The further retrievers advance into high-level work, the more likely confusion becomes. By striving to achieve nearly absolute control on blinds, while promoting good marking coupled to an excellent hunt, we open the door to a host of undesirable reactions.

Rarely is there a simple answer to advanced training problems. Some solutions may be achieved by thinking the problem through; others resolved only by experimentation.

The key to problem solving is to stay acutely tuned to your dog's nature and reactions to your efforts. Remember, any course of action can be abandoned when it becomes clear that it is without benefit.

Advice is often given by friends of both amateur and professional standing. Listen to advice, put it in the hopper, and act on it if it seems appropriate. More likely, though, after you have had years of training experience, your reading of your dog is going to be the most accurate.

Don't be surprised if an offbeat training maneuver produces excellent results with only one dog. We've trained dogs whose hunt was significantly improved by handling on marks, allowing more water cheating than is usually condoned, or permitting such faults as switching or returning to old falls to disappear on their own. When such training methods work we conclude that the dog involved is significantly different from the norm. In most cases, other, more conventional approaches are successful.

Many adolescent dogs exhibit behavior that requires improvisation. Willingness to shake off absolutes and devise methods more applicable to special cases is advantageous. For example, there might be an ideal time in the life of a "typical retriever" when force-fetching, sitting on the whistle, or steadiness should be achieved. When and how to work on these phases of training varies. Some dogs respond well to most standard methods, and will come close to learning on a set time schedule. Many don't.

This book is not a complete compendium of methods designed to remedy all retriever problems. The approaches that we suggest are based on cases of dogs we have trained. Trainers vary as much in their personalities and aptitudes as their dogs. As a result we cannot guarantee that methods we have found useful—or not—are going to produce similar results in the hands of all trainers.

The demands and expectations that trainers apply to their dogs reflect not only their idea of what constitutes a well-trained retriever, but also the level of the sport in which they are involved. Field trial or hunt test dogs face established requirements. The hunter may see those requirements as necessary, or not.

Great latitude exists, depending on the owner and his interests. We hope this book will provide ideas for solutions to problems and inspire the reader to become a resourceful trainer.

CHAPTER 1

BASIC OBEDIENCE

MANY OF THE PROBLEMS arising in retrievers that have had some training involve a breakdown in obedience. Obedience commands must first be clearly taught, then generalized to the situations where they are needed, and then, as training progresses, the desired standard must be upheld. Laxity or omission of any of these steps can result in poor or sloppy responses, and difficulty in further training.

Although constantly riding herd in an uncompromising way is counterproductive, certain absolutes must be maintained. Foremost, a retriever must come when called, and do so without a lot of wasted motion in the process. Unless a dog can be recalled promptly, and reliably, there is little you can do to remedy problems as they come up. Many dogs, even some of those already trained as retrievers, are either unreliable on the recall, or return in a reluctant, indirect fashion. As the dog comes to realize that the "Here" com-

Coming when called is essential.

mand is not consistently enforced, his response to it deterio-
rates further.

In all cases, failure to come readily is frustrating and inconvenient for the handler, making beneficial training harder to
achieve. A failure to come can also result in serious injury or
death to your dog. The applications are obvious: calling your
dog from a busy road; preventing fighting with another dog;
drinking or eating unsafe water or food; and the like.

Teaching dogs to come when called is straightforward.
Those who have already been taught to come may profit from
a refresher of the type they had in early training.

With a youngster who does not thoroughly understand the

concept of the recall, we use a rope of 20' to 50', depending on the training site. You do not want a long rope if you're training where there are lots of trees, bushes, or other obstacles that may entangle the rope. Initial work can be started in your living room with a 15' cord. We prefer polypropylene cord as it floats, untangles easily, and doesn't pick up as much dirt as nylon or cotton clothesline.

We usually have our students wear the e-collar during these procedures, but attach the cord to a snug-fitting chain choke collar. We do not activate the collar, or use shock during the first phase of training.

It is a good idea to let the youngster roam more or less at will for a time, investigating the area, lifting a leg, and so forth. When you feel your dog is used to the territory, and the presence of the cord, give your recall command, usually "Here" or "Come." Some use the dog's name as an attention getter before the recall command is given. As soon after the command is given as possible, give a sharp jerk on the cord and guide him in. A few applications of this will have your dog turning quickly and coming to you.

If your dog has already been conditioned to the e-collar on the "Here" command, you can start by working with the collar. Use no stronger a nick than is necessary to achieve a prompt response. Practice several sessions to instill in this "trained" dog the necessity to obey the recall command. Be prepared in the field to keep responses sharp; if you don't they will return to the form that caused problems in the first place.

With the youngster on his first time through recall training, you have the opportunity to do a better job than those who require remedial work. In most training, the first time is the best time to erase uncertainty.

When your retriever is responding quickly to the cord, after a few sessions' practice, the time has come to activate the e-collar and administer a light but attention-getting nick with the same timing that you used with the cord. The cord should still be in place on the dog's choke collar. If the desired response is not achieved by the application of shock, immediately follow up with a jerk on the cord. Once the pupil shows quick response to a nick with the collar, the cord jerk can be

Training on recall with long line and e-collar.

eliminated. Leave the cord attached for a few more sessions until your dog demonstrates complete understanding of the recall command.

Next, "generalize" the command by practicing it, with collar enforcement, in a variety of locations and around tempting distractions. Practice in training- and hunting-type locations with wild animal scent, training group meetings with other loose dogs as temptations, and other places in which you can instill the responsibility to come when called. Be aware that calling a dog away from another person can create confusion. Retrievers sometimes interpret "here" as meaning "run to the nearest person."

Occasionally a dog will bite when given a collar correction for hanging around a stranger. To train your dog to come to *you* when you call, use well-instructed helpers in a controlled situation—don't do it in public places, around strangers or children. Tell your helpers to ignore your dog if he runs to them. Use the long cord in conjunction with collar correction to make your dog see that the "right answer" is to come to you.

Several other commands follow the recall in general usefulness and are in our opinion essential to a well-trained retriever. "Sit," "Stay," "Down" (as in lie down), "Get down" (as in don't jump on me), "Kennel" (get in the kennel, load up in the car or boat, etc.), and "Heel." If your dog understands, and quickly obeys, these commands, disobedience should not stand in the way of other training.

If your dog fails to obey smartly, the fault could be in any of several areas. The dog may not understand because of skimpy instruction on the command, or because he thinks he is supposed to do something else. He may be inhibited because he has been punished in the past for what he thinks you are now commanding him to do. If, after teaching the command in your house or yard, you did not practice in more challenging settings, he may think it does not apply. If you have tolerated a poor standard of response in connection with retrieving, he might think that is acceptable to you. Finally, his willingness to comply may be poor, although we suspect fewer dogs are in this category than most owners think.

A program that will address most of these causes is to review the command starting in the teaching stage, review it again in a typical field training setting (and others if you wish), and then set up some very simple, short retrieves in which you focus on the standard you now require. If the retrieve is not challenging, no harm should come to his other work from your corrections on obedience—and you won't be tempted to overlook infractions in an attempt to promote a successful retrieve. Once his performance is reliable, gradually increase the demands of field work, maintaining established obedience standards.

The reinforcement of additional obedience maneuvers is uncomplicated. The same pattern may be applied as was implemented in the recall. Teach each new command by physically forcing your dog into the desired position until he is familiar with it. Then add correction, using the e-collar, training stick, or a jerk on a check cord, to achieve a transition from physical force. In cases where the e-collar is not to be employed, the trainer must be able to reach the dog in order to enforce commands.

If, during the "training review" and generalization stages, your dog appears overly hard-headed, there are two approaches you can try. Sometimes retrievers, particularly Labs, can tune us out if our corrections are not stiff enough. Physically insensitive individuals can shrug off the means we use on most dogs. The first method is to increase the level of correction. This will either work quickly—within one or two corrections, after which you can return to the former level— or it won't work at all. Don't persist if you don't see rapid improvement, as undue harshness may cause trouble in other areas.

The second approach is to make the good things your dog has come to expect contingent on his proper response to commands. We presume he likes to retrieve. If you tell him "Sit," and he does not, don't call for the birds. After a time, force him into a sit, call for the birds, and let him retrieve. Let him understand that the new rule is that he must sit on command in order for the birds to be thrown. Most dogs are eager enough to eat that you can apply the same principle at feeding time. Teach him he must sit to receive his supper. Then, if you like, you can teach him to remain sitting until you release him, or you'll snatch his supper away before he can eat.

A proper sit is needed for drill work, marks and blind retrieves.

The "Sit" Command

The "Sit" command is essential during marked and blind retrieves. It must be obeyed immediately without fidgeting as the dog remains sitting. Sitting improves steadiness and attention, which helps to promote positive marking. On blinds, or marked retrieves in which an infraction calls for sitting in response to the whistle, the dog is put in the ideal position to receive commands—solidly facing his handler in a sitting position.

Teaching the "Sit" command should begin with the cord attached to the choke collar, and the un-activated e-collar in place if it is to be used. A jerk upward on the lead coincided by a push downward on the dog's hips should make him sit. With many youngsters, you may have to hold your dog in the sitting position until he gives up struggling to get up. Once he accepts the sitting position without physical force, use your training stick and time a smack on the rump with the "Sit" just as you timed the rope jerk with the recall command. With some dogs, a sharp upward jerk on the lead and choke collar will work in place of the training stick. Experiment.

When your dog responds well to the "Sit" command, introduce the e-collar with a sufficient nick to get results. Practice remote sits frequently, insisting that a short blast on the whistle, or the command "Sit," means sit immediately and don't move until further notice. Your efforts will be rewarded if your retriever comes when called and sits any-where on command.

When training FC-AFC Jaffer's Blackie I was surprised to see that he had already learned to sit on the whistle with near absolute reliability. His owners had practiced this from puppy-hood while taking him for walks. A single blast on the whistle meant sit and stay until called or given a "Hie-on" release com-mand. The result was wonderful and it carried over into his formal blind training beautifully. If your dog is already well trained, but is slipping in the area of the "Sit" command, schedule some sitting drill sessions for him and keep at it reg-

Enforcing the "Sit" command with a training stick.

ularly until you see improvement in the field. Don't accept a lower standard in the field. You don't have to cream the dog for failures, but do interrupt the retrieving lesson and insist on a good response before proceeding. Desire to get on with the retrieve is sufficient motivation for most retrievers to sit properly, if you are consistent.

The "Stay" Command

"Stay" is a command used by some trainers to communicate emphatically to their dogs that they must remain in the sitting or "Down" position until released, even if their handler is out of sight for prolonged periods. Some trainers contend that "Stay" is redundant, that "Sit" means sit, and "Down" means lie down, until you are given another command. We think dogs can learn proper behavior either way; they are probably less concerned about the choice of words than their trainers, who can argue the point for hours. We use "Stay" with young trainees when we anticipate that they might do otherwise: when we leave them sitting and walk away, for example, or the first few times we open their dog box and want them to learn not to jump out until released. Soon they learn to "Sit" until told otherwise, and to remain in their box until cued to jump out.

Heeling

Heeling is an essential in all working retrievers. There are many cases where a dog should be required to walk quietly by your side on or off lead without the necessity of nagging commands. We find the lead and training stick to be useful in heeling exercises. If your dog consistently wants to forge in front, as many eager retrievers do, use the stick to tap him on the nose, or the cord to sharply jerk him back. The e-collar can be used in place of the jerk or the stick once the command "Heel" is fully understood.

While teaching heeling, the handler should frequently come to unexpected halts, requiring the dog to stop and sit without command, then to resume heeling when the handler moves on. The dog, while heeling, should be constantly tuned to his handler's movements, neither pushing in front, nor lagging behind. The dog's head should be even with the handler's knee.

If a trainer responds to his dog's errors by accommodating them, slowing down as the dog lags, or hurrying as the dog forges ahead, the dog's heeling will become sloppier as the trainer compensates for his mistakes. On the other hand, a trainer can improve a dog's heeling by doing the opposite—exaggerating his mistakes. Correcting small errors amounts to nagging, and may confuse and discourage the dog, or cause him to avoid heeling position. Taking advantage of his inattention, exaggerate the error, then correct. This clarifies the lesson. If your dog starts to get ahead, slow down, increasing the gap, then suddenly stop. A good correction is a jerk up and backward on the lead attached to the chain collar, propelling the dog back into the sitting-at-heel position. We say, "Sit" during this operation, even after the dog has learned to sit automatically when we stop.

Step forward briskly to exaggerate the dog's error and correct.

If the dog lags behind, the trainer steps up the pace, again opening a gap. A collar nick accompanying the command "Heel" works well to teach the dog to keep up.

Proper heeling is done with the head up, not sniffing the ground. Elimination of ground-sniffing is essential for attentiveness and overall quality of work. A difficulty lies in the fact that many dogs react to correction by lowering their heads.

We have developed an indirect approach that works well with most dogs. Instead of nicking or jerking the head up, whenever a dog's nose goes to the ground, we stop suddenly, say, "Sit!" and give a solid sit correction. The correction may be a nick or a jerk—whatever has been established as an effective sit correction with that dog.

Heeling for extended periods of time in the field, or under the excitement of competition, requires more than a few short practice sessions in the yard. Practice heeling on long walks, or controlled heeling in tempting circumstances, according to your needs. If your dog creeps or beats you to the line, see our chapter on "line manners."

Heeling properly can have a profound effect on the quality of a retriever's work. Some field trialers have claimed that 75 percent of winning is related to a retriever's behavior between the holding blind and his arrival on the line. Deterioration of heeling will result in a decline of overall performance while hunting or competing.

Practical applications of heeling are numerous. While walking up birds, the dog at heel remains in a position to see game flushed, so he is in a good position to mark. As stated, he will remain at heel in the sitting position until his handler gives the command to retrieve, thus freeing the handler to concentrate on shooting. If the dog does not heel properly, he will most likely be out of position for steadiness and marking. Preparation for flushing should include the excitement of live birds and shooters.

If you have a dog that is inclined to fight, you have an especially important need to teach heeling with certainty. While hunting, or competing in trials and hunt tests, your dog will have many close brushes with other dogs. An iron-clad command to heel may prevent a dangerous fight that could result in costly litigation or expulsion of your dog from formal events.

The "Kennel" Command

Does your dog always enter his kennel, crate, car, or door to the basement when ordered, or does he hang back, looking for a way out? If he is of the latter persuasion, teach the command "Kennel." This is best taught with three commands: "Here," "Sit," and "Kennel," in that order. The "Here" command brings him to you, the "Sit" puts him quietly under control until you want him to enter the desired space, and the "Kennel" command propels him into whatever you wish him to enter.

A tap from the training stick can help teach a retriever to jump on his own.

Usually, the command to "Kennel" will involve your dog's being put in a familiar and comfortable setting such as his crate, a car, kennel, and such. Occasionally, the command can be used successfully to encourage your dog to enter a new place, such as a strange truck, or perhaps a boat, if he has not been in one before.

We have found that bodily propelling a dog into his crate (or car, etc.) is the most successful way to teach this command. Sometimes it is necessary, as in cases with truck beds that have to be jumped into, to assist the entry for a number of repetitions before a dog will jump in on his own. Be patient and use the "Here," "Sit" as a preliminary to gain control.

We have had many dogs resist jumping into their boxes on the dog truck, but readily jump into the lower dog trailer. After jumping into the trailer a few times, they willingly jump up into the truck. We don't know exactly what is so hard in the first place—is it not seeing what they were jumping into, or lack of confidence in their coordination to jump into a relatively small opening? We just know the result—as with many impasses in training, breaking the problem down to a simpler level allows for quick mastery.

There is no need to make the "Kennel" command entirely a matter of force. The use of a treat, biscuit, etc. tossed into the enclosure you wish him to enter simultaneously with the kennel command may be useful.

Obedience won't make your retriever a great performer, but, no matter how much talent a dog is born with, he will not achieve greatness in the absence of obedience. Almost all dogs, over a period of time, show some loss of sharpness in their response to simple commands. A regimen of obedience drills in addition to maintenance of standards in field training will help prevent backsliding.

COLLAR-WISE
by John

BILLY WUNDERLICH, in his assessment of the e-collar as a training device for field trial dogs, once said, "These dogs aren't stupid—they know when they don't have it on." This implies that if dogs wear the e-collar constantly in training, they will be aware of its absence while competing in formal events. This awareness may result in the dog's becoming "trial wise," a condition which results in a breakdown in reliability under judgment.

Collar trainers, which practically all of us have become, argue that dogs become so habituated in their behavior while wearing the e-collar in training that the control thus achieved carries over into competition. It should be remembered, though, that field trial dogs spend a lot of time in training and a very small amount in competition. If the proportion were reversed, the e-collar would not be as effective a tool for training as it has become.

Capital City Jake was five when I took over his training. He had a problem with his water blinds—giving in to temptation to land where he shouldn't, a common failing. I had decided to train Cappy without the e-collar, since the work he had done under collar training had not produced satisfactory results. I was unable to get a decent water blind out of Cappy without the collar. Every other area of his work was in good shape. One day, I decided to try a water blind that had given him particular difficulty with the e-collar on. The result was amazing. He ran the blind perfectly, on and off the point of land for the second entry and then out to sea in rough water.

This was an eye-opener. Cappy knew how to run the blind, including what temptations he could not give in to with impunity, while wearing the e-collar. I had to find a means to train him to do a good water blind without relying on the collar.

I accomplished the task, at least marginally. My most effective tactic employed a product known as a scare cartridge. These 12 ga. cartridges, which can be fired in any shotgun, launch a projectile with very little report upon firing. When the missile is about 100 yards out, it explodes with a loud bang equivalent to an M-80 firecracker. A couple of these shot over Cappy's head at the strategic moment of infraction convinced him he'd better behave, e-collar or not.

Once Cappy would do a water blind in the absence of the threat of the e-collar, his performance in field trials become competitive and he quickly earned his FC and AFC. Some of his water blinds were spectacular, while at other times he fell into the old pattern. Such faults are rarely eradicated, although as Cappy's story shows, they may be improved.

CHAPTER 2

MOUTH PROBLEMS

WHEN THE SUBJECT OF "mouth problems" is mentioned we are apt to think first of that bane of the retriever trainer's job—true hard mouth. This trait is characterized by immediate crunching of the bird's bone structure, and likely eating the bird, upon finding it. This condition is quite rare, but occurs enough to be of concern. Note that little puppies frequently bite down hard on birds, and grow out of it—see the chapter on Puppies for details.

Retrievers are distinguished from many other dogs with strong hunting and pursuit characteristics by their gentle mouth. A retriever that destroys game, rendering it unfit for the table, is useless no matter what his other attributes may be.

Hard mouth, like most other traits, comes in varying degrees of severity, but the end result is the same. The game they return to you is no good. The question can be asked, is it possible to train an inherently hard-mouthed dog to be soft-mouthed? We doubt it. The condition may in some cases be brought under control temporarily, but the cure is usually only marginal, with a strong tendency to recur. Further remedial measures will be called for, and the final result is usually typified by the individual's final slump into a lifelong habit of mishandling his birds. The message here is to identify hard mouth as soon as you can in a young prospect. If you intend to train through it, do so at an early age, when your chances of success are greatest.

A thorough program of force-fetching is the only method we have seen to have success with hard mouth. Often the degree of training required in these cases is beyond that which the dog can sustain without damage to other areas of his work, such as marking, style, or motivation. Too much hazing and force usually carry with them consequences in other areas.

Rarely will a dog that has shown a gentle mouth throughout his early training switch to hard mouthing birds. Other mouth difficulties can arise, however, as a result of carelessness in training, such as allowing sloppiness to creep into bird delivery, using old and decomposing birds or birds that are badly shot up, too infrequent exposure to birds, and so forth.

Training mistakes are better headed off than dealt with after the fact. The more firmly established the bad habit, the more work will be needed to overcome it. For mouth problems, the treatment generally starts with close-range work, with the dog at your side or on the force table. Then comes a phase in which the dog is eased back into field work (and drill work, if that is where the problem appeared), and care is taken to maintain good mouth discipline. We use this approach for most mouth problems: keep work simple at first, increasing distance and challenge at a pace that enables your retriever to maintain his new discipline and you to remind him as needed. This pace will be rapid for some dogs and will require considerable care and time with others.

Let us address a few of the most common mouth problems.

Roughing Birds

Roughing birds is a frequent problem with dogs of a playful nature. Usually, there is no hard biting of the bird involved, but the end result can be similar to that of true hard mouth. The bird will be rendered unfit to cook, with torn skin and lacerations in the flesh.

The best treatment we have found for this problem is a quick reprimand, on the spot of the infraction. This generally consists of a verbal scolding such as, "No, No, You hold that bird, Hold, Hold!" This is accompanied by forcing the bird into the dog's mouth, sometimes well back toward his throat while repeating the command "Hold!" The command to hold, of course, must have been taught in conjunction with his earlier work in force fetching.

Often, a couple applications of this kind of correction, accompanied by a few yard lessons on holding, heeling with bird in mouth, and prolonged sitting and holding sessions, will settle the issue. Keep a sharp eye for its reoccurrence in the

Obedience drills with birds help establish proper bird handling.

future and address it immediately if the tendency persists. We have had a number of experiences with dogs who have been permanently cured of roughing their birds with only one on-the-spot correction.

Soft Mouth

Quite a few retrievers, particularly those devoid of strong field trial breeding, have mouths that may be described as too soft. These dogs often mess with their birds excessively before picking them up, drop and readjust their hold continually on the return, and are inclined to drop the bird before you are able to take it from them. This is particularly aggravating when a crippled bird is involved and it goes fluttering off before you are able to get your hands on it and dispatch it.

With dogs that display an inadequately firm and aggressive grip on their game, some remedial work on force fetch is usually required. Long holds, heeling with the bird in mouth, and associated measures may help, just as they do with the rough handling sort.

With many dogs that are tentative about bird handling, the cause is lack of exposure. Retrievers are not all born with an equivalent desire to pick up and hold birds, especially birds that are still alive.

When we receive a trainee with a wimpy mouth we generally kill some pigeons fresh and give plenty of retrieves with birds that are palatable and easily handled. As the enthusiasm increases, larger birds and live birds can be added. As with other mouth problems, excessively soft-mouthed dogs should be trained on birds with regularity throughout the year. Don't just trust to luck when the hunting season comes around.

Slow Pick-up

Some dogs, although their mouths are exemplary in other respects, do not pick up their birds promptly. Exactly what the reasons for this phenomenon are, we don't know, but we strongly suspect training errors (usually too much pressure).

If an individual has been harshly corrected for bird roughing,

Establish good bird handling with gentle practice on "Hold" and "Leave it."

that could be the cause. An excess of birds in bad condition could be another. Large cripples, like geese and pheasants beating and clawing at the dog's face, might be another. We trained a field champion Chesapeake whose pickup had been perfect, but after a winter of goose hunting, during which he was repeatedly corrected for not picking up large geese, his pick-up became painfully slow. He was dropped from one field trial as a result of standing over birds for long periods before picking them up. It was a good call on the part of the judge. Even though the rest of his work had been excellent, no one wants to see a field trial competitor who is reluctant to pick up birds.

Probably the most reliable cure for this condition is to lighten up the training demands and recreate enthusiasm for birds through the use of shot fliers. If your dog originally displayed a penchant for cripples and runners, shackle some live birds and give him an abundance of chances to chase down his game.

When you return to your normal regimen of training, try to keep tuned in to the reappearance of the slow pickup and what might be causing it in your training methods. In young dogs and puppies who have not had many birds, a hesitant pickup usually is a result of inexperience. More birds will usually help.

Formation of associations is an important aspect of canine learning. A dog may form associations with a particular situation that lead to apprehensiveness. Notice if your retriever does a better job in one situation than another. Work to establish a good pickup in the situation where he does well, then gradu-

Be lenient if at first your dog doesn't deliver large or unfamiliar birds.

ally add elements of the other situation, maintaining good work as you broaden his favorable associations.

In a few cases we have known, slow pickup reappeared from time to time in field trials. This happened with FC Banjo XXXVI. In one trial Banjo won, she sniffed at and rolled on the final bird before picking it up. Apparently, the judges forgave her for this as they awarded her with a win. They asked, at one point during this display, "What is she doing?" I replied, trying to cover for her, "Oh, just adjusting her hold." They accepted this explanation, but would have been within their rights to severely penalize her.

Freezing

Freezing (not releasing the bird to his handler) is the second most difficult condition to address, behind true hard mouth. In most cases, retrievers who freeze do little damage to the bird. They simply clamp down tightly enough so you can't extract it from their mouths. Usually, the harder you pull, the firmer they hold.

We once saw a humorous incident in which a retriever refused to give up a pheasant at a field trial. The handler took the bird by one leg and pulled until the leg came off. Surreptitiously, he slipped the leg in a pocket. It went the same with the second leg, leaving only a legless pheasant that was finally rescued from the dog's mouth by dint of sheer force. The contestant then handed the dismembered fowl to the judge who asked as the handler left the line, "By the way, what are you going to do with those legs?"

Even though freezing is a daunting problem, often showing little promise of a cure, we have had some success dealing with it. The bird, or the bumper, whichever the retrieved object might be, can be viewed as a kind of security blanket in the case of many dogs who have received too much force. They feel they have completed the job by getting the bird in mouth and fall into an almost trance-like state as they refuse to let go.

Pressure with the e-collar or other means at this point often produces a result counter to that which you want. A nick with the e-collar, rather than making the offender release his hold, often has the effect of making him clamp down tighter. We have found that a new form of corrective pressure, which will essentially surprise the dog rather than inflict pain, will sometimes do the trick.

Hold a short dowel or piece of broomstick concealed at your side, then bring it up rather sharply under the dog's chin with one hand while you place your other hand gently on the bird to receive it; this approach will sometimes work. Beating on the dog to gain a release will rarely work—just a single tap will do.

Some dogs will freeze purely because they love to hold birds and refuse to give them up. This is especially true of field trial dogs who realize, after a certain number of retrieves in a test (say, three) that the game is over and so is the fun. The tap under the chin works in some of these cases. We suspect that you can get away with only a small number of these corrections. They may get the dog's attention, but consistent work to practice good delivery is needed to follow up. Once the surprise is gone, the taps will probably be no more effective than other failed methods of correction.

We have known of handlers who tried methods such as concealing a thumbtack point up under a band-aid on the tip of a finger, and jabbing the dog under the chin when the command to release the bird is given. The same technique has been attempted with the use of a burning cigarette applied under the chin while grasping the bird. Techniques such as these, while painful to the dog, were not in our observation successful.

Some advocates of 100 percent e-collar training (including the force fetch) use electric stimulation both on the command to take the retrieving object and to release. This has proven to work in some cases. Overall, however, the likelihood of creating confusion, even exacerbating the freezing problem, seems to present a greater risk than the potential benefits. There are always risks to using the same form of reinforcement for opposite behaviors such as "Hold it" vs. "Leave it" or "Drop."

Fidgety or Nervous Hold

A mouth defect that is regarded primarily as an aesthetic failing but often develops into a worse problem is the fidgety, or nervous, hold. This syndrome is characterized by frequent and rapid, almost spasmodic clicking together of the jaws while holding a bird, particularly upon delivery.

Some dogs have an unsettled and nervous nature from birth, but in our observation, the fidgety mouth is frequently the consequence of incorrect or incomplete force fetching, the dog being normal in other respects. If left uncorrected it can lead to freezing and sometimes hard-mouthing the bird. We have seen both results.

There is usually a high level of anxiety or fear in the dog who spasmodically mouths the bird when delivering. The behavior does not appear to have conscious motivation, but is more reflexive, almost like a nervous tic.

Obviously, relaxation is the key to correction of this fault. We think a return to the force fetch program is required in these cases. Usually a dog so afflicted will grab the dummy quickly on command, as that part of his force fetching has often been accomplished with too much pressure.

We recommend very light pressure followed with praise and

stroking as your student holds the dummy. Make your hold sessions generous but not tediously long, and repeat the fetch, hold, praise sequence over a period of five to ten minutes. Use verbal correction (a quick "ah!" for rolling or chomping the dummy) and praise for brief periods of quiet holding, to help the dog understand the distinction between what you want and what you don't. Be patient, as your dog is working to overcome an established habit. Repetition is needed. Sometimes physical correction, in the form of a firm chuck under the chin accompanied by a reminder to "Hold," will clarify the picture for the dog, but sometimes it will feed the dog's anxiety and hence his compulsive mishandling of the dummy. If one or a few physical corrections do not help, leave them for the time being and work with verbal corrections and praise alone.

With many, if not most, difficulties encountered with retriever mouths, the problem is more with the handler/trainer than it is with the dog. In several cases we have seen dogs with mouth problems go to a different training environment only to have the problem abruptly disappear. Some trainers' dogs rarely have bird-handling problems whereas others seem to be plagued by them.

We have taken in training quite a few dogs with chronic mouth problems. Nothing seemed to have worked for the owner-handler. Frequently, the problem disappeared quickly while we were training the dog. Usually no particular corrective methods were employed, just work as usual. We admit that a high proportion of these "cures" backslid to their previous level when they returned home. This suggests that features of the handler's style had affected the dog's delivery. If an owner seeks help from a professional trainer or skilled amateur, the most important phase of the instruction often consists of a change in the handler's approach.

Without having watched all of these owners extensively, we can't say for certain what aspects of their handling were at fault. We try to handle dogs in a manner that allows them to be more relaxed. We have noticed, in general, that we are less absolute in our daily requirements for the dogs. As mentioned in the obedience chapter, we uphold standards for certain trained responses, but we allow dogs to make mistakes while applying their learning to new situations. We also work to keep our actions predictable from the dog's point of view. We design training set-ups with an eye to possible errors the dog might make, so as to avoid sudden and harsh corrections over principles that are not part of the current lesson.

Many almost great, and some great field trial retrievers have had moderate to serious mouth problems throughout their lives. The wonderful NAFC-FC Dee's Dandy Dude had a playful mouth as well as an inclination to stick or freeze on the bird. His owner, Mike Paterno, dealt with it as best he could. There are videos of Dude returning with birds in a National Amateur trial, which he won, showing him rolling birds on the ground and repeatedly picking them up and dropping them as he returned. Paterno carried a rubber ball in his pocket to ensure that Dude would release the final bird in a multiple marking test. The idea was that his dog would anticipate the play time with the ball after leaving the line, thereby encouraging him to willingly give up the bird.

Black Gum Gus was a dog who could have achieved greatness except for his habit of sticking on birds in trials. His trainer, Earl Kimball, tried every trick within his expertise, and while it appeared at times the problem had been cured, it continued to crop up at times pivotal in the dog's career.

Be prepared for the inevitable. Like a bad hand in cards, it will eventually come around. Still, we have experienced only two cases of incurable hard mouth for which nothing worked, although we have seen a number of marginal successes. Most of the other problems we see with dogs' mouths are a result of a combination of inheritance and poor training. You can't do much to change a dog's breeding, but you can do everything in your power to direct your training program toward a desirable end.

GALE

A CASE THAT ILLUSTRATES many of the points in this chapter is that of a Chesapeake bitch called Gale. Gale came to us fairly young but already showing a nervous mouth, allied with an excitable nature. Her early training focused on teaching her self-control, and we put extra effort into being low-key and predictable to avoid contributing to her tendency to become "higher than a kite." Before moving on to the force part of force-fetching, we did extra work on "Hold," first getting her to hold dummies and birds quietly and properly, and then working her on obedience routines with a dummy in her mouth.

Gale proved to be tough-natured enough to take training pressure well, but we were still careful of the amount of pressure and length of sessions so as not to evoke a reactive, apprehensive response to the "Fetch" command. She completed her basic training and proved to be a hard-going, never-say-die type of retriever and an excellent marker, although always at risk of getting carried away by excitement.

After two or three seasons, Gale came back to us with a mouth problem. She was refusing to give up birds, and sometimes eating them. As often happens, the problem was worst on smaller birds, her handling of mallards and geese being good. We started her remedial training with a review of "Hold" using plastic dummies. We continued with mallards and then to the more challenging pigeons, getting her to hold them properly while heeling around the yard and doing short hand throws. Applying the method of increasing challenge gradually while maintaining good behavior, we went to short retrieves in the field, still using pigeons, then longer and more challenging ones, then shot fliers. By the time her owner came to get her, she had had one or two flier pigeons a day for a month and had handled them flawlessly.

On pickup day, we demonstrated Gale's perfect delivery on a long flier in the cover. Then her owner handled her on a second flier. After she returned, when commanded to "Leave it," she refused to let go.

We selected the "momentary" setting on Gale's e-collar, advised her owner to tell her to "Sit," and accompanied the command with a medium nick. When he repeated "Leave it," she released the bird. After one correction, she properly delivered a number of short hand throws. We sent her owner home with freshly-killed pigeons and instructions to start at short distance, increasing as we had done. His presence (which was connected to her poor deliveries in the past) constituted an additional challenge.

We learned the following Spring that Gale's deliveries had been excellent all season. She remains, however, a high-maintenance dog that requires calm handling and benefits from bird-handling refreshers at the start of each season. Indirect pressure on the sit command while she was already sitting proved an effective means to boost her owner's credibility so he could begin a program of bird handling work with her.

CHAPTER 3

NO-GOES

YOU PUT YOUR HAND OVER your dog's head and say "Back!" He sits there, motionless. Perhaps the biggest failure in a retrieve is not to start the retrieve on command—the No-Go—the dog equivalent of the racehorse that doesn't leave the starting gate.

We rely upon our retrievers' natural desire to retrieve, but only to a point. Some dogs, of course, lack sufficient ambition. Often no-goes derive from that deficiency. The phenomenon will occur, however, in almost all dogs that are carried through advanced training. The causes are many, and varied. No matter how hard going a dog is, he has a break-down point at which the unpleasant aspects of training pressure outweigh his desire to retrieve. No-goes occur in most dogs even though they have been thoroughly force fetched, forced on back in yard and water patterns, and so forth. One of the most critical aspects of training is to be able to see these break-downs coming, and to know

*What we expect when
we command, "Back!"*

what to do when they happen, and, of course, to head them
off if possible.

It could be said that a dog that doesn't go when sent is
incompletely trained. True, but it must be noted that, complex
as training has become, it is not always easy to know when the
point of overload has been reached.

Usually, the symptoms leading to refusals to leave the line
are pretty easily read. Apprehensive starts, failure to focus on
the object, and a worried demeanor upon approaching the line
are all signs that your dog is losing initiative.

The most obvious treatment for the no-go is not to let it
happen in the first place—lighten up on corrections, decrease

Watch for signs such as a worried demeanor when coming to the line.

complexity of tests, and shoot more fliers. This approach is often commendable, but in many cases may constitute a reluctance on the part of the trainer to see a task through that inevitably must be confronted.

Suppose your dog is a well-trained three-year-old who has had the basics properly instilled when a youngster, and has always taken off enthusiastically when sent. Then, suddenly, he doesn't. For starters, with this dog, you need to review the nature of your training sessions, and ask yourself the following questions. First, and most importantly, has the level of corrections in the field, that is, after he has been sent on a retrieve, greatly counterbalanced the pressure he has been receiving behind the line, that is, before he is sent? It is axiomatic that when training through no-goes, training pressure such as the stick or the e-collar, when given behind the line, produces better results than corrections administered after leaving the line. Although from early training on collar reinforcement has been used to propel him toward his objective while he is moving, reducing this form of pressure may help.

We have found, in forcing on back, that restraining the trainee on a cord while giving a couple of nicks with the e-collar, or swats with the training stick, is more effective than running out and giving the same correction after the dog has been sent. The psychology you want to build on is this: the worst thing he can do when sent is remain on the line. The rewards lie out in the fields and water.

You want your dog to know that the rewards lie out in the fields and water.

So, let's set up an actual situation, one most trainers have encountered many times. You send your presumably well-trained dog to retrieve, and he sits there like a dummy. Do you blow up, jump all over him while cussing him out? No, we hope not. Don't repeat the command if you are sure he heard you. Back up, take the dog off line in a calm and deliberate manner, put a short polypropylene lead and choke collar on him, and heel calmly to the line. When reaching the line, com-

Pressure "behind the line" with e-collar and short cord.

mand "Sit," then back up a step or two, heeling your dog with you, then administer pressure while restraining your charge from going and simultaneously repeating the command "Back." Then release him to go when the message is clear and he's struggling to go.

For dogs that have been properly forced on back in the yard, this is a refresher course and will be quickly understood. It won't work, of course, on those who have had improper or incomplete basic training, and those individuals should be given the benefit of that training.

You will find, though, that dogs that have been thoroughly forced in the yard will rarely benefit from returning there for remedial work, as they are unlikely to give you a refusal in the yard. It is better to do your corrections on the spot while working on the kinds of tests that are giving your dog trouble. This will convey the message, "No matter how daunting this test looks, don't even think about refusing to go as the consequences of that behavior are more unpleasant than anything that will happen to you after you have left the line." This adjustment must be accompanied by a commensurate reduction of correction in the field. Fewer call-backs, e-collar, or other corrections while working on the retrieve are mandatory. You are readjusting your priorities, at least until the likelihood of no-goes has been reduced to near zero.

The level and type of correction employed for no-goes is an important matter. Most retrievers will happily sit on the whistle or come when called in response to the mildest level of e-collar corrections or a light tap with the training stick. Forcing on back, when the no-go occurs, however, requires elevating the level of pressure to the point of discomfort at which the dog clearly fears a repetition. We don't want to abuse our dogs, of course, for humanitarian reasons coupled with the knowledge that excess heat can ruin the dog. What we are looking for is the exact level of intensity that will accomplish the desired result, and no more.

Dogs vary greatly in their susceptibility to pain. What hurts one goes practically unnoticed by another. If you give the big, extra-tough individual a couple of smart whacks with the training stick while repeating "Back, back," and he acts as though you were commending his misbehavior with a love tap, the level should be raised. On the other hand, if the timid, soft dog reacts as if overcome by panic, you have probably gone beyond the limit.

We have found that the variable strength e-collar is most beneficial for extremes of toughness and softness as the impulses can be regulated all the way from barely noticeable to quite painful. The choice of a momentary versus constant mode, too, can be useful in finding the proper level of correction for your dog. At the upper end, you will find few dogs that are insensitive to the top level of correction on constant mode.

The training stick works well on some dogs. In basic training, we apply force with the stick before the e-collar is employed. There are lots of fancy training sticks available, some of them selling for $20 and more. Pick one you like, but make sure that it is stiff enough to get results with a moderate swat on the meaty part of the rump.

Administering corrections with the stick can be difficult with certain dogs. "Pudge," FC Oakhill Exponent, was so fast and evasive that it was almost impossible to give her a whack. When she saw it coming she would dance about. Wherever you swung, she wasn't. It's a good idea with such dogs to get them under control and use the e-collar. In Pudge's case, I merely heeled her to the line after the no-go, stopping every two steps and giving the command sequence "Sit," nick, "Sit," then sending her when I reached the line. This worked on her.

If you reach an impasse on no-goes with an otherwise hard driving dog, you might examine the demands you are making with the tests you set up. A couple of examples come to mind.

Maintain the dog's expectation of success.

Several years ago, we were attempting to teach a friend's dog a difficult marking concept. This triple consisted of a long dead bird to the left of a thick island of cover in a field of cut corn. The second bird was thrown into the thick cover directly in front, and retired. The third bird was a flier deep and to the right of the island of cover. Our training friend tried repeatedly to do the test as a triple, though we suggested he break it down into singles. The dog could not remember the indented retired-gun throw in the island of cover. After a tediously long and excessively tough session the little female completed the test. That was, most likely, enough, but her handler wanted to follow with a blind brushing the right side of the island of cover. The result was a series of no-go problems that were hard to correct.

Pudge began to give no-goes when I [John] was trying to teach her to take a small corner of water honestly. Her reaction was, one, to run around the water staying dry, or two, take too much water. The issue was getting under my skin. Soon I found myself frustrated and taking a hard line, berating the dog and not helping either one of us. Fortunately, I saw the writing on the wall before it was too late. Pudge began with the no-goes and a generally disheartened attitude toward her work. I said to myself, "Oops! I'm making a mistake here. I'm in the process of ruining my dog." I made the right choice by ignoring the no-goes and removing the corner-of-water drill from her repertoire. The result? Pudge was as honest as she needed to be for competition, sometimes overly honest in the water, but, if a little cheat was needed to do a tricky water mark, she would do it. One of her wins was aided by the fact that she wasn't so honed out of cheating the water that she couldn't nail a mark down the side of a muddy bank near the water. Most dogs failed, because their training dictated entering the water whenever they got near it.

Whether your dog is inadequately prepared, or an apparently well-trained individual who is backsliding, you will have to plan to reduce the demands of test difficulty and correction first, then raise the bar, so to speak, until you have passed the point that aggravated the problem. Incremental training is essential. Don't expect the problem to disappear overnight. Be steadfast, however, and don't condone no-goes by sending a second time. Vary the strength of your corrective enforcements, but keep them ready. Be calm, methodical, and reasonable in your demands, and corrections. Steady pressure over the long haul will help solve problems that sudden trauma will exacerbate.

REAL
DOGS

MAGGIE

by John

S OMETIMES, CORRECTIONS FOR problems resolve themselves in a unique fashion. Maggie's problem of no-goes in the water on long entries (50 yards and more) had reached a particularly difficult phase. She was a hot little Labrador bitch loaded with excess drive. She had been properly forced and put through an adequate yard program as well as forced in the water from short to moderate ranges. When I tried longer entries, though, she balked. I thought I had done nothing wrong in her early training, yet there was no denying the problem.

After trying the usual cures I struck on a method that worked. We don't usually use long cords as a method of forcing on back, or correcting no-goes. My opinion of cords for this purpose was based on failing efforts I had experienced with their use. I had observed, on the contrary, that hauling dogs on a cord almost always produced negative results. Occasionally, however, a short length of cord laid out in front of a dog in the direction of the mark or blind appeared to propel him toward his objective. Often this could be enhanced by giving a couple of forward jerks just before sending the dog.

Employing an extension of this approach, I purchased a 200-yard roll of white polypropylene cord, which floats well on water. I attached one end to Maggie's collar and put the other end in the hands of a helper 200 yards away, hidden on the far side of the dam. On signal my helper jerked on the cord as I sent Maggie. If she hesitated anywhere along the course of the line to the water, I raised my hand as a signal for another jerk. After a small number of repetitions in a variety of long water entries, I was able to do without a helper. I stretched out the cord on the desired route before running Maggie. Then, I clipped the cord to her collar, sent her, and she followed the line directly to the dummy. She literally "took a line."

Soon I got good results without the line. Maggie won two Qualifyings and finished an Open. In the twenty years since training Maggie, I have not treated "No-Goes" with the long-line method.

CHAPTER 4

LINE MANNERS

A FELLOW FIELD TRIAL TRAINER once commented, "Most trials are won within ten feet of the line," the line being the spot in front of the judges from which dogs are sent. There is much to be said for this point of view, considering the numerous problems that can arise from poor line manners and their consequences in the field.

The deterioration of work in competition has its counterpart in hunting. Take marking. As your dog bobs and jumps all over the line, he creates an unfavorable impression on the judges, and loses precision in marking. Bad manners while hunting are a nuisance in the blind, and interfere with marking, assuming you can get any shots while trying to hide with an overactive dog.

Whining and barking while birds are being shot are grounds for dropping a dog in field trials and are unacceptable while hunting.

Poor line manners and lack of control go together. The

Good line manners are needed whether competing or hunting.

likelihood of your dog's engaging in a fight with another competitor is increased as deportment fails. We find that most line-manner failings stem from poor obedience, but are often not successfully treated with conventional obedience training. It must be remembered that sports involving birds shot over dogs' heads place the students in a provocative situation. If everything has been done to gain control through excessive obedience training we may have cut off our noses to spite our faces. That is, we may raise the level of physical correction to the point that it backfires in other important areas. Although sometimes risks must be taken to achieve an end, training should be gauged so the solution to one problem doesn't create another.

The question of establishing line manners involves a delicate balance of forced repression while trying to maintain maximum initiative. In watching dogs at work, many carry the mark of having been downtrodden by an excess of control improperly applied, or worse, of permissive laxity. Either end of this spectrum fails to produce the qualities most desirable in a working retriever.

Usually, poor behavior on the line, or while approaching or leaving the line, is to some extent compartmentalized—your dog has special occasions when you lose control and he takes over. We don't like to resort to psychology in explaining this behavior, since we have only a layman's understanding of the field, but the principle of sublimation seems to cover some of these breakdowns of control.

Sublimation is the repression of behavior patterns at the expense of a buildup of pressure that ultimately will be released. It can be likened to an over-inflated tire. If the pressure gets too great, it's going to pop. Rex Carr said, paraphrased, "every dog and man has a breaking point." If pushed far enough, they will respond with unwanted behavior.

This is a valuable thought, suggesting that it is preferable not to take an ironclad stance with regard to dog training. We get on particularly shaky ground if we are absolutists on the subject of line manners, and might be better off out-thinking our dogs rather than overpowering them.

Consider the dog that knows everything there is to know about heeling, but cannot resist beating his handler to the line by distances varying from a few feet to several yards. He has learned, one, that he can get away with it, and, two, that he gains a certain relief from built-up pressures resulting from control of his behavior. Probably, harsh coercive measures will do more, with individuals of this type, to build up pressure than they will to solve the problem. In many cases, the breakdown that occurs as a result of repressing the desire to beat the handler to the line is worse than the original one. Suppose it takes the form of barking and whining or breaking when the birds are shot.

In the case of Dual-AFC Capital City Jake, the cost of getting to the line in an orderly fashion, which was by no means guaranteed, was sometimes a display of outlaw behavior when leaving the line. Such items as failing to leave the line at heel, attacking bird crates, knocking them over, or initiating a fight with the dog coming to the line were all in his repertoire. Cappy was immensely talented, but had such an overload of desire that his inability to contain it curtailed a possibly great field trial career. On the other hand, when taken hunting, Cappy was a model of exemplary behavior. Why? Possibly because the pressure of competition was off.

So what can we do to decrease the pressure on the dog who is about to bubble over? Probably, we need to construct an activity that will on the one hand satisfy the need of an outlet for built-up pressure and on the other eliminate all rewards associated with the undesired behavior. This approach precludes beating your dog into submission, an action that may be tempting at the time, but that will only worsen the problem.

First, let's remove the reward for unwanted behavior. Suppose you heckle and harass your dog every trip to the line with the slingshot, training stick, voice commands, or whatever, yet the dog continues to beat you to the line. Obviously, the dog's lack of manners indicates that he has accepted the physical correction as a "small price to pay" for the pleasure he derives from making the retrieve. You have in this case reached a state of equilibrium with your dog that is not likely to change.

If we remove the physical correction on the trip to the line, replacing it with a single verbal command to heel, then allow the dog to beat us to the line, we will have the same situation as before, but leave out the corporal punishment. What then? When you arrive at the line, quietly place the chain collar and lead on your dog and leave the line, dog on lead, at heel, with no retrieves.

If nothing else you will have gotten his attention. What's up? No retrieve! Once he makes the connection that beating you to the line, no matter how tempting, is a no-win proposition, you have removed the reward for unwanted behavior. Compliance carries its own rewards as noncompliance its penalty.

If misbehavior such as beating you to the line or creeping has become established, it may take extra work to get the dog to make the connection that line manners are his passport to the reward of retrieving. Not only must you withhold the reward for poor manners, you must find a way of getting manners good enough to reward, so your retriever can get the idea. This may mean simpli-

"Creeping"

fying the retrieving setup and making it as unexciting as possible—perhaps a short, single, dummy throw with no shout or shot. If you can get him to the line, and sitting quietly during the throws, you can establish the contrast between the manners that procure the chance to retrieve, and those that don't. Once the connection is made, a few setups at intermediate levels of difficulty and excitement are needed before he is working at his former level. Be prepared to turn and head for the holding blind or truck the instant he slips.

If you get only an approximation of manners at first, don't despair. When working with rewards, it is possible to increase standards. If you get an improvement over what you started with, take that as your new standard and gradually raise it once your dog has the idea.

The next step might consist of something to satisfy the dog's excess energy. More work is a possibility—exhausting long swims, difficult tests, all designed to create the impression that this is fun, but also hard, tiring work.

Many problems of line manners can be treated in this way. If the motivating force is the prospect of getting the bird, make that conditional upon proper deportment. Be consistent about withholding the reward when your dog misbehaves, and he is likely to learn to "do what works."

Vocalization at the line, as we have said, is a severe flaw. We have had success getting rid of vocalization simply by application of the calm, predictable handling style described here and

Do not allow your dog to retrieve until he lines up properly.

in Chapter 2 on mouth problems. We have rarely had to face a vocalization problem head-on. If called upon to do so, we might try making the retrieve contingent upon silence, similar to the approach used for creeping, beating us to the line, and so forth. The challenge is in making the dog realize that silence equals the right to retrieve.

A couple of years ago we obtained a puppy, named Flower by our daughter, from a bloodline known for vocalization problems. We trained Flower to be quiet as we brought her supper. If she let out a yip, and later, even a whine, as we carried her feed pan across the yard, whoever was feeding her turned away, saying "Stop the noise!" and walked out of sight. She learned to be quiet in anticipation of feeding, and to respond correctly to "Stop the noise!" in a variety of circumstances. Flower's training was interrupted and recently resumed. We do not know yet whether her understanding of "Stop the noise!" will be sufficient to get her to be quiet on line. Keeping quiet at feeding time has proved such an effort for Flower that by the time her pan is set down, she is too excited to eat. When released to eat, she laps compulsively at her water, then waits a few minutes before eating her supper.

On the subject of repressed behavior, FC/AFC Ch. Warpath Macho had a strong desire to hunt on his own. With dogs of this type you will probably not be able nor want to discourage this hunt. Sometimes a session of indulging misbehavior will remove the bottled-up energy resulting from its suppression. Macho won an Open All-Age stake and made his field championship following a four-hour deer chase in the pine barrens of South Jersey. He had escaped control while airing and came back at about noon, only fifteen minutes before his number came up to run the first series. He appeared tired and scratched up from the chase. Despite his fatigued condition, he ran a near-perfect first series, and continued brilliantly throughout the trial. You wouldn't intentionally risk your retriever on a hazardous deer chase, but in this case it may have put Macho, who was overly keyed-up, in condition to win.

One of the most important elements in field trial or hunt test dogs, and to a lesser extent, in gun dogs, is the ability to sit quietly and move with the handler in the direction of the birds as they are thrown. Many retrievers fail to pivot with the handler to improve their view of falls.

The chief requirement for pivoting with you is steadiness. Some dogs get the notion that, if they are allowed any move-

Because he is under control, we can help him on the memory bird.

ment, the sky's the limit, and they begin creeping. The pivoting maneuver can be taught with a wagon wheel pattern. The dog is taught—yes, you may move with me, but you're not to go until sent. Most dogs are intelligent enough to learn this lesson. Conduct it slowly and carefully to prevent St. Vitus' dance on the line.

It is actually possible to slide by in field trials, winning and placing in some, with a dog that has loose line manners. So long as the dog doesn't break, bark, or beat you to the line too badly, most judges are apt to allow you to continue if the work is otherwise good. This does not mean that you should settle

After he gets the basic message, a "sit"-nick-"sit" reminds him to contain himself.

for poor line manners. Rest assured, you will pay for weaknesses in this area with commensurately poorer performance in the field.

A good model of line manners is the calm but attentive dog who can successfully be lined up for a retrieve by the handler's hand held over the dog's head. If your dog is jumpy, and not really steady, the approach of your hand to his periphery of vision might mean "Go!" You can insure steadiness if you put your hand over your dog's head and delay the command to retrieve, "Back," or the dog's name, "Brownie," not allowing him to go until the voice command is given. Some dogs learn to respond to very fine adjustments in the direction they are sent by working with the hand over their heads. Your dog must be very secure on the line, however, to accomplish this.

Other dogs line up with the handler's body position. No hand is used, but the dog is re-heeled, or pivoted, until his attention and back-bone are aligned in the direction you intend him to take. Although some handlers use this technique on blind retrieves as well, its main application is on marks.

It bears repetition: unless your dog arrives at the line of competition in a calm, collected manner, you will not be able to help him much. As Jay Sweezey once said, with respect to influencing the dog's direction on marked retrieves, "They all need help."

BLACKIE

FC-AFC JAFFER'S BLACKIE HAD run a beautiful trial, but returning with what he thought was the last bird of the final series of water marks, he turned to leave the line. He had forgotten the retired-gun pheasant thrown in high cover on the opposite side of the pond. When he turned to leave, I said, "Blackie, heel." He returned to the line, sat down, and soon remembered the forgotten fall. When his ears came up with recognition, I put my hand down over his head and said, "Back." He swam a straight course across the pond and disappeared into the cover. Motion of the tops of the cover, and occasional glimpses of Blackie's tail, showed his progress toward the mark. As he turned with the rooster in his mouth, I heard a judge's book slam shut behind me. Judge Mary Howley said, "Well, this trial is over." Her co-judge allowed that she was considering a fifth series for a tie-breaker. Mary answered emphatically, "I said, this trial is over."

Blackie's willingness to cooperate combined with his ability to be helped on line made this win possible.

CHAPTER 5

LACK OF HUNT

RETRIEVERS ARE BRED to hunt. With some dogs, however, an intelligent and relentless hunt is not inherited. Failure in hunting can also be caused by training confusion and excess pressure. Marks, and blinds, for that matter, are executed more effectively by dogs with enthusiastic hunts than by plodders. Rarely, in a difficult situation, does a dog land precisely on the downed bird. The dog's knowledge of when and where to stop, honoring his nose when he reaches the area, bringing the search to a quick conclusion, is his most valuable asset. Get the bird!

Puppies often reveal an intense hunting instinct at seven or eight weeks of age. Some even show effective use of their noses at that age. Other puppies who show little of this skill early in life develop into fine hunters with age and experience. Some don't. First, we would like to deal with the problem of dogs who show little instinctive hunt, but seem otherwise talented.

We must admit that we find it disheartening when we

A persistent and productive hunt is a retriever's most valuable asset.

come across an otherwise promising dog who lacks hunting vigor. At the same time, dogs in this category present an interesting challenge, and if given the proper encouragement, and exposure, may develop hunts that range from adequate to good. Rarely will a dog with a naturally weak hunt attain the level of hunting brilliance exhibited by the great NFC-AFC Mi-Cris Sailor, who looked better hunting a mark than most dogs do stepping on it.

Probably the worst thing that can befall a young retriever whose hunt is defective, is failing a large percentage of his marks. The student may conclude that he's no good at finding birds and give up trying. This downhill course can be avoided by making sure that his success ratio on marks is high—for a time pushing 100 percent. Success breeds success and the promise of a better future.

Still, little or nothing has been done to develop an energetic hunt, but the seed has been sown—the green dog thinks he will find a bird, or dummy, when sent. We do not subscribe to the notion that hunts can only be improved by shooting lots of birds over the dog. In some cases, a lot of birds will get them going. In many instances, however, following the force-fetch program, there is so much enthusiasm for getting dummies that they seem to work just as well in developing the hunt.

We start our marking training with obvious throws in which the hunt is not challenging—white dummies in short grass, or short throws in the water. As the retriever progresses we make use of higher cover in which the dog must put on a short hunt. The distances are generally modest, as trying to increase range and improve hunting ability simultaneously is usually counterproductive. We make our early marks in the cover short, which creates an assurance that he can get it quickly. When he fails to step on it but puts on a quick search, ears up, tail wagging, we are seeing the beginnings of hunting.

Often dogs with little or no hunt will give up when the first birds or dummies are thrown in cover. The dog will often give a quick look and return to you, or in some cases, stand still and look for help. If this behavior is allowed to continue, the problem will grow worse, and the likelihood that you can deal with it effectively diminishes. Helping the dog that will not persevere by handling, or re-throwing the marks, usually leads to dependency on assistance.

This golden's hunt is developing nicely.

The next step in improving a dog's hunt should be, again, to make it easier. Sometimes a large white dummy that can be seen more easily, or moving to sparser or shorter cover, will help. As the weeks go by, providing your dog has a high interest level, you should see improved commitment to hunt the dummy, or bird, with fewer quits. As he improves, gradually increase the length of marks in cover. The density of cover can also be increased.

We tend to think of retrievers as having indomitable spirits and the gameness to go on no matter what obstacles are encountered. It is true that many individuals among Labs, goldens, and Chesapeakes show this trait. Excessive challenges, however, rarely contribute to the hunt.

There are certain environments that are best avoided altogether. Thickets of blackberry brambles, bull briars, and dense entanglements are more likely to discourage dogs than to "toughen them up." We have seen forbidding cover employed in field trials to separate the sheep from the goats, so to speak, but the dogs who approach such encumbrances with a positive attitude are more likely to succeed than those who are bludgeoned with such obstacles as a daily routine.

We have access to some ponds that are unusable in midsummer because of the density of water plants. At that time of year we retreat to more open water. The point is to keep demands within reason. The great performer will have plenty of opportunity in the course of hunting and competition to deal with extra tough environments without overexposure in training.

There are a wide variety of techniques used to enhance dogs' hunts. Most of these work as a temporary boost, but cause side effects that may grow into serious problems if overused.

The walking bird method is sometimes used to excite the retriever who has a too laid-back hunting style but can be revved up with live birds. The procedure is straightforward. The dog must be steadied and allowed to watch a pigeon with clipped wings disappear into thick cover. The dog can be steadied for varying lengths of time, allowing the bird to work its way deeper into the cover, promoting a more difficult search.

This method, though sometimes effective, can backfire if it is pursued to the point of dependency. We can think of a parallel in training coonhounds. Many trainers, and we tend to agree, feel that hauling a coon up a tree to encourage young hounds to bark treed should be done little, if at all. Making a task too easy can create a dependency on easy tasks.

Another useful crutch is to use a live shackled or pinioned duck or pigeon on marks. Live game usually generates excitement and drive, positively affecting the hunt. As in the previous example of the "walkaway," live birds are easier to hunt up than dead ones and will elevate the incidence of success. If you want to re-use your shackled ducks, though, don't throw them as hitting the ground will kill them. Plant the bird and throw a dirt lump to the spot. When he gets there, there's the bird!

Salting the area can be a good gambit, particularly on longer marks in which you are trying to improve the hunt. This consists of spreading several retrieving objects, usually

You want your retriever to approach the area of a mark expecting success, and maybe a bird.

dummies, over an area of ten yards or so in diameter. If your dog makes it to the area he is likely to have success after only a brief hunt. In many cases this will improve a dog's attitude on the longer difficult marks, resulting in a more positive hunt.

If your dog tends to break down on long marks and shows little or no hunt, "feeding him" dummies on his way to the area can be useful. In this method, the helper, or automatic launcher, is used to throw additional dummies as the dog is on his way. This is strictly a confidence builder on longer marks. Avoid extensive reliance on it.

We have had little success forcing dogs to hunt, and we daresay, although we use force when required, rely on it less than some other trainers. We think that talent comes first and training second. Of course, you can't do without either. To return to the subject, it is possible to remind well-trained, collar-conditioned retrievers to stay in the area and hunt. In this method, quitting, or returning without the bird, is addressed by a collar correction, getting the dog sitting and under control, and handling him back into the area of the fall. Training of this type can be intimidating to the retriever and frustrating to the handler. It is a useful tool only in skilled hands. We have seen many competitive retrievers who have been trained to hunt in this way but appear cowed and panicky while hunting. In competition, we see much less of this today than we did twenty years ago.

Carrying hunting demands to the extreme characterizes the method we will call the "Birdless Mark." In this method, which is related to the previous method, a mark is thrown—but not a retrievable object. A lump of dirt that disintegrates upon hitting the ground is a good example. The dog is sent and allowed to hunt for varying lengths of time until the thrower flips him a bird or dummy when the dog isn't looking. The dog then finds the bird or dummy. We haven't seen impressive results from the use of this technique. In some circumstances, however, the birdless mark, enforced with collar correction and handling back into the area, may be what is needed to lengthen the duration of the hunt.

At a different level, we have found that forcing on back sometimes improves a dog's hunt when a long program of marks designed to be encouraging has not worked by itself. Then, if the dog returns without the bird, apply pressure and re-send him.

Occasionally we see evidence that a dog is not using his nose effectively. It seems reasonable that a dog that doesn't know how to respond to scent might not expect to find a hidden dummy or bird. Most of these dogs have a perfunctory hunt. Most Labs, goldens, and Chesapeakes have good enough scenting ability to do their jobs, and our experience is that dogs can be taught to use their noses to find birds.

One procedure is to get the dog to use his nose to find his dinner. Make up a dog's feed and hide the pan in light cover. Take the dog for an off-lead walk in the area, approaching the hidden feed from a downwind direction. When you see that he is beginning to catch the scent, try not to distract him as he works it out. Encouragement is not needed, as he gets the reward of supper. It is amazing how inept a young retriever can be initially. Fortunately, in a few sessions they learn quickly to follow up scent, and develop the expectation that they can find something if they hunt for it.

As we mentioned, some dogs appear to have their hunting ability or inclination compromised by training. We have seen novice trainers who are mainly focused on gaining and maintaining control, or who work primarily on blind retrieves. It can also occur when a softer dog is exposed to an absolute training program, or when dogs are frequently handled on marks they do not "pin." The solution is usually increased marks with less interference and a high success rate. If the dog is not fearful of correction, he may come around quickly.

Too much handling on marks or blinds can harm a dog's hunt.

We trained with a British field-trial bitch that had always been handled on her marks. She was a good, aggressive retriever and soon learned to find her birds without help. A worried dog may need a longer program. In general we recommend keeping blinds and control training in balance with marking and initiative development. When the vigor of a dog's hunt declines, it may be time to adjust the proportions in each department.

The substance and improvement of the hunt lie in fostering increased confidence and enthusiasm. Many retrievers have marvelous natural gifts. Some of them are deficient in one area, such as hunt. We try to bring out the best in weak areas as well as strong ones.

JADE

by John

TARHEEL JADE WAS MY FIRST field trial winner. Puppies we consider competitive prospects today have more going for them than Jade or they are sold as started gun dogs when their weaknesses become apparent.

Jade was a nice puppy, intelligent with a strong retrieving instinct. She was also one of the last "grandchildren" of the history-making stud dog FC/AFC Paha Sapa Chief II. I had high hopes for her. Her first defect consisted of an absolute abhorrence of water, which I will not elaborate upon here.

Jade was a pinpoint marker, devoid of hunt. Her early training consisted of easy throws in short grass. When she was about six months of age I took her to fields of cover—sparse grass calf high. To my disappointment she revealed what was to become her downfall in field trials. If she didn't pin the mark, she gave up, stood there, and looked at me.

Over the years, until I sold her as a gun dog at age eight and a half, I tried to improve Jade's hunt. Although she won a 105-dog Open Stake and qualified for the National that year with an additional second place, I could never sufficiently improve her hunt. She got a number of green ribbons and a fourth for a total of eight and a half Open points in eight and a half years. I hate to think of the number of trials she could have won if she had given me a half-decent hunt in the final series. I will admit to some handler errors that cost her her title as well, but I am sure if I had been able to improve her hunt I would have made her Field Championship several times over. Making good guesses when to persevere and when to take a new tack is an important part of success.

CHAPTER 6

LACK OF STYLE

THOSE OF US WHO HAVE observed many owners training their first dogs would probably concur that the most common error is pushing too hard—too fast. The results of over-accelerated training are almost always negative. Confusion, failure to assimilate attempted lessons, and last, but far from least, loss of style are the likely by-products of rushing training. I [John], at least partially, learned my lesson while training my second Chesapeake, Pilot, some fifty years ago.

I was in the process of struggling with a 150-yard water blind that was over his head. I was anxious to show my training partners, all with years' more experience than I had, that my year-old dog could do the same blind their more experienced dogs had just done. As my demands grew more insistent, Pilot became increasingly reluctant. My training partner, teacher, and mentor, Bob Johnson, said, simply, "You're getting too ambitious." Being a youngster, it was news to me

Good style enhances our enjoyment of our retrievers' work.

that ambition was not necessarily a plus in all situations, but, brief as the criticism was, it sank in.

Of course, we would like to head off an accumulation of bad training habits before it results in a loss of style. Unfortunately the early signs are easily, and often, overlooked. Your dog may look at you confusedly, do double-takes, or hesitate when being sent before the problem is full-blown. Then, suddenly, he starts moving half-speed and tail down, with a downcast demeanor. If this happens, you have a problem requiring attention. The longer you avoid addressing it, the more entrenched it will become. The result may be a dog whose work is permanently damaged.

Style can be an indicator of the clarity of a training program.

Before discussing cures for a loss of style, let us say that the basic style level in retrievers is inherited. Some move quickly, energetically, and happily. Others fall somewhere between stylish and pluggish. There is probably little you can do to dramatically change the inherent nature of the dog. Some improvements in style can be expected among most retrievers given excellent training.

Another issue is just how much style you need or want. Watching a variety of top trainers will reveal some interesting information regarding style. At the top, in our opinion, you will see trainers whose dogs exhibit exuberant style combined with a high level of cooperation and control. At the opposite extreme, you will find trainers who have reduced their dogs to the "sleep-walker" level of lack of style, whose work may be precise and highly controlled. This latter type has given way to the former in recent years. We are glad to see the trend. There was a period twenty-five years ago when some accomplished field trialers asserted that fast dogs were a thing of the past.

Style should not necessarily be equated with speed. Some slower dogs have a lot of hustle, try hard, and appear up-beat and positive. A few dogs appear to be overly screwed down, ridden with anxiety, and unhappy with their job, even though they go fast. In general, though, a decrease in your dog's speed is accompanied by loss of style.

Whenever new material is presented, such as the poisoned-bird blind in which a bird is thrown or shot and the retriever is required to pick up a blind retrieve first, a slowdown and some confusion are inevitable. Of course there are some individuals, the geniuses of the breed, who take all new lessons in stride, never missing a beat. One was FC/AFC Jaffer's Blackie. In the fifth series of the Open at which he made his title in 1977, the tie-breaker series consisted of a double blind and poisoned retired shot pheasant. Blackie had never seen the test in training or trials, but nearly lined both blinds and pinned the mark. Don't hold your breath until you get one like him.

Almost all retrievers require carefully administered step-by-step training on technically difficult tests to avoid loss of style.

Continually plunging ahead with the "I think I'll see if my dog can do this" attitude is generally ineffective. Build through gradual increments in difficulty, not dramatic leaps.

There are many steps that one may take to improve a dog's attitude and hence, his style. One of the most useful, and least used, technique is the "break." This is particularly true if you are a relentless taskmaster by nature. We all need a vacation at some point, and your dog is no exception.

A needed break can take several forms. One is simply to lay your dog off for a few days. Lessons that have been too hard-taught, or traumatic in terms of correction, will sometimes be forgiven with a few days' rest, and the desire to work can be rebuilt through inaction. This is especially true if your dog is allowed to watch others being worked from the confines of his kennel or training vehicle. I have seen many dogs bounce back after a few days of confinement following a harsh training session. Sometimes it will appear that a dog who has had particular difficulty with some lesson will come back from a rest with work that seems to say, "Oh! I've got that now."

The "break" can also take the form of lightening the training regimen. This can be temporary, or more or less permanent. We determine the level of work tolerance as we train. Less is often better, whereas more intensive training may plunge them into a downhill slide.

Sometimes it is worthwhile to redirect the workload emphasizing your dog's strong points. A spill-over occurs in which the dog's success on things he does well positively affects

Accepting delivery from the front lessens the burden we place on the retrieve and may improve style and confidence. Sitting to deliver is easily re-established.

those he does poorly. Like other "lifts," this one has limited application and should not lead you to retreat from stickier problems. Tarheel Jade, who was a training lesson in herself, loved blinds, particularly difficult water blinds. She was intelligent, knew how to do them, and exhibited a restoration of confidence whenever blinds were the assignment.

Jade was unusual in having a preference for blind retrieves, but it originated in her fear of missing marks because of weak hunting instinct. She became progressively less stylish if worked extensively on multiple marks, but her style improved when she ran more blinds. Possibly her style would have been better if we had concentrated more on blinds and limited her marks to shot fliers.

A higher percentage of dogs will be "brought up" by marks than by blinds. When dealing with a particular dog, however, percentages don't count—the preferences and idiosyncrasies of individuals are what you have to work with. Make the most of their talents and work to deemphasize the weak points.

If your dog's style improves at field trials or hunt tests, but he's pokey and indifferent during training, introduce some of the excitement factors that occur at events and look for a positive response. Keeping him in a holding blind while another dog works will pep him up. Some dogs may rev up when they hear the marshal call out the running order. Consider every possible device that might give your dog the impression that he is at a field trial or hunt test. The presence of a number of other dogs on the grounds can make a difference as well, so try to train in groups whenever practical.

We have had experience with a few dogs that work beautifully, and with acceptable style, on their home turf, but become apprehensive and pluggy when away from home. Of course, the more limited your training grounds, and the more exclusively you use them, the truer this will be. Even if you have a mediocre range of training sites available, different scenery introduced on a regular basis can improve style in new settings. If your dog is an extreme homebody you may have to do a lot of driving to provide him with enough varied settings to improve upon the problem. Some dogs never get over the sagging style response to new territory. The majority of dogs have more adaptable personalities and perform well in most settings.

The style of many dogs improves with praise. Praise is commonly given to excess, either cracking the dog up or completely boring him. The cracked-up dog becomes unmanageable and the bored one indifferent. A light scratch behind the ears and a calm "good boy," or sitting on the tailgate, dog at your side, quietly hanging out can result in positive style responses.

House-raised dogs are, we think, usually more stylish performers than strictly kennel dogs. That doesn't mean you have to sleep with them, although if that's your bag it probably doesn't do them any harm. A regular program of house time is conducive to the development of style. How much you are willing to put into this is a matter of personal preference. Other style enhancing "togetherness" programs may include walks, car rides, etc.

Frisbees, balls, and freebie dummy throws are often employed by trainers, especially amateurs, in an attempt to jolly their dogs up and improve style following hard work. We think the chances of this working to your dog's detriment are greater than they are of helping him. Often, horsing around after a teaching session seems insincere. If any animal is hard to con, it's a dog. We recommend leaving the line in a controlled and sedate manner. Of course, if you've just won the Open, have at it; it's not going to happen often enough to make a difference.

We don't think free play with other dogs is a constructive way to address a style problem. We also think that being allowed to roam at large is counterproductive, and dangerous. Confinement in the kennel and dog truck tends to build a dog's desire to work, and improves style. Using the tie-out chain to allow your dog to watch others work will help develop enthusiasm in some cases, but not all. Some will lie down and go to sleep.

Nutrition and health are factors in style. A dog can't perform at or look his best when being nagged by health prob-

Better discipline may be the key to style.

lems. Some interesting research is being done regarding stamina and feeding regimens. In brief, feeding high-potency food once a day, after work is done, is thought to promote endurance. Before adopting such a program, however, we recommend that the reader investigate the subject in greater depth than we can provide here.

There is yet another side to building and maintaining style that we refer to as the "wake-up call." These methods involve the imposition of various forms of discipline on the flagging retriever who is slipping into increasingly lackluster performance. Several of the foregoing techniques may help these dogs, but some need to be reminded of their responsibilities in certain terms.

In many cases, obedience drills will produce noticeable benefits. A session of Heel, Sit, and Here will often cause lazy, slow behavior to be replaced with vigor and enthusiasm. A dog responding in this way seems to say, "Good, I'm back in the old groove. I was concerned with Jim's slipshod training lately!" Dogs, in order to perform brilliantly, require clearly defined standards. High standards build confidence.

Some dogs show a lack of style only in certain areas. More often than not, style difficulties occur around water. Many retrievers are not especially water-inclined regardless of what we read about them in breed descriptions and standards. In addition, many water tests we prepare for today are ambiguous—*should I get wet now or later? Should I get out here, or there? Cross at this point or that?* the dog asks in a mire of confusion. Water style suffers quickly when the requirements are not made clear.

Force, properly applied, and made absolutely clear, almost always increases style in the water, even in a weak water dog. Force may be electronic or old fashioned. Both work. If the force is just punishment, however, it will have a negative effect on style.

We have worked out a few basic requirements in the water that can simultaneously bolster style and lay the groundwork for more technical tests.

High-flying leaps are fun to see but may be dangerous.

First, the dog must get in the water when he's sent. This is foremost among rules regarding water. Second, the dog must take whatever obstacle comes up on his path to a water objective—points and islands may be boarded in course and the water re-entered on the far side. When channeling we teach the dog to stay in to the end, then as marks or blinds are placed on the sides of channels, dogs can be taught to deal with that. If these principles are made clear, subject by subject, your dog will comply happily and become a more stylish water dog.

Early in life, FC/AFC Burnham Buff would not hit the water with style. Her owner, Paul McGee, a neighbor of John's at the time, lived on the shore of Cedar Lake in Minneapolis. She was a talented yellow bitch, but walked into the water. Roger Reopelle recommended throwing dummies off the end of a dock for her, presenting a choice—fall in or jump. She chose to jump and soon developed a good water entry in other settings.

We do not tamper with dogs whose water entries are acceptably brisk but do not involve a leap. The spectacular leap is fun to see but is also hazardous. Dangerous obstacles may exist just below the water's surface. Landing on them has caused serious injury and death. If you have a spectacular leaper, examine the water sites you train in carefully.

As your dog ages, the exuberance of youth will start to fade. Some dogs maintain marvelous physical condition throughout their lives, and you, who are entirely in control of their diet and exercise, are in a position to extend their well-being and style as far into life as possible.

Decreasing workloads, less exposure to cold water, warm housing, regular workouts, and adequate nutrition are all keys to health and longevity. Your dog's style will serve as a barometer of the requirements and adjustments you make as he ages.

DUDE

ANY TOP FIELD TRIAL, hunt test, and gun dogs have had excellent style, but when I think of style my thoughts go back to the great NAFC/FC Dee's Dandy Dude. "The Dude," as his owner/trainer, the late Mike Paterno, called him, was anything but speedy in his old age, but he continued to win. Fast as a young dog, Dude became increasingly arthritic with age. Still, when sent his ears were up, tail wagging, and he was clearly happy to be working even though it was painful for him to rise from the sitting position when sent to retrieve. "The Dude" had a stylish mind and a big heart coupled to an indomitable spirit that made him, in my book, one of the most stylish retrievers ever.

CHAPTER 7

DIRECTNESS

FIELD TRIALERS HAVE STRESSED the importance of developing straight lines going to and returning from their objectives. To the casual observer, and some trainers of gun dogs, this requirement may seem unnecessary and overworked. Practical experience in the hunting field as well as in successful field trial campaigning reveals the reasons for this emphasis.

A well-executed retrieve will be conducted without undue disturbance of huntable cover. Straight-going dogs concentrate on their objective, not on their route, marking more effectively. Valuable hunting time is saved through speedy recovery of downed birds.

Some dogs appear to be born with a tendency to go straight and are easy to teach that direct lines are a requirement. Other dogs seem to have a detouring nature and never take a direct line to anything unless rigorously trained to do so. The majority fall between these extremes. They show some directness in their work accompanied by an inclination

On puppy marks, make sure the straight route is the easiest route.

to avoid obstacles causing them to lose momentum before reaching the area of a fall. Early training undoubtedly has an effect on dogs' tendency to go straight. Building enthusiasm and speed in young dogs by restricting range and avoiding cover or water challenges that may throw them off line is a good start. Water marks for puppies, as well as land marks, should be direct and square to the obstacles they encounter so the youngster can't figure an easier way to his retrieve than going straight ahead.

Puppies and young dogs should be run on marks of limited difficulty to reduce confusion as to their location. Large white dummies, white pigeons, and short cover are some keys to making the mark obvious, decreasing the tendency to wander.

We have used various techniques to improve lines. These

procedures will vary in effectiveness according to the receptiveness and training level of the dog.

Dogs who have been trained from puppyhood without cheating temptations, and are progressing well, reach a stage at which honesty can be challenged in small ways.

Polypropylene training cords of different lengths can be useful for early lessons in going straight. Let's assume you have reached the point at which you would like your dog to go straight in the water. Once the dog is swimming, half the battle is won. Select a body of water that has a mild cheating temptation. Avoid strictly parallel down-shore retrieves at this point. Have your mark thrown (a big white dummy) by a helper—not too long. Expect your dog to slide down the shoreline avoiding a direct entry.

The instant you can see that your dog is committed to running the shore, stop him with the cord and bring him back to the line. Move up a few steps and repeat the mark. Most hard-going young dogs will quickly understand that the retrieve will be permitted only by a direct water entry. This result can generally be achieved in a few sessions, but establishing a reliable habit takes longer. As with most phases of training, however, once good habits are formed, slippage can be treated with relative ease as the dog's principles have been established.

Each phase of honesty or directness training is treated in this way so as to make the rules crystal clear to the dog. Tendencies to rush through cheating problems too fast, or increasing difficulty too quickly, are probably the mistakes most commonly made by beginners.

The next step we take in training for direct lines employs a helper for hazing. Hazing consists of harassments of the dog on his way to an objective, making it more pleasant to go through obstacles rather than avoiding them.

An example we do with most dogs, usually before one year of age, is to have a helper thrash the water along the edge of a channel with a cane pole to prevent the dog from running the shore. Some settings require a helper on both sides. How well this works depends to a large degree on a dog's drive. It also hinges on the severity of hazing. You don't want to spook your dog out of the retrieve, which can occur with softer dogs and those who have not been forced on "Back." This technique can be administered to some inexperienced prospects who have not completed their basic training. Many youngsters respond to hazing with aplomb even though they are months away from completion of formal basic training.

In conjunction with the use of the cord and hazing, "feeding" bumpers as the puppy is on his way to the mark can be useful. When using a helper, have him keep a half-dozen dummies in hand. On signal have him say, "Hey! Hey!" and throw a duplicate mark. In many cases this will urge the youngster back on the line he was losing.

As your dog comes closer to taking reliably straight lines you can begin to make greater demands. All dogs have a limit, of course, and effective training avoids going beyond their abilities. Make the most of what they have. This is the crux of well-balanced training—what to do, when to do it, and how much to expect. Some dogs of low intelligence reach their peak potential when force fetched, steady, and delivering to hand. With such dogs, your expectations for sophisticated work will not materialize. Be satisfied with a clean retrieve.

Intelligent dogs will often surprise you with their ability to quickly pick up even the most subtle routines. Be careful with geniuses, however. They, too, require habit formation on all phases of training.

When training has advanced to the point at which these "conventional" methods of teaching straight lines are exhausted, with technical water and long entries, you are ready to move on.

Before going farther, the basics should be complete. If you have an older dog who has not had adequate basics, you must do whatever you have missed or risk confusion. Basic training consists of "Here," "Sit," and "Heel." He should respond to the whistle or voice for "Here" and "Sit," even at a distance. Force-fetch, forcing to a pile, handling on the yard pattern and, in the water, swim-by, should be complete. Then he should be ready for handling corrections as he attempts to avoid obstacles.

If your attempts to handle your young dog to the correct route on a retrieve fail, your problem is with handling more than with honesty.

Handling through obstacles can be more difficult for the trainer than for the dog. The key is clarity. Suppose you nick your dog as he approaches an obstacle that has flared him off line. He is apt to get the idea that the obstacle is the cause of his discomfort, not the fact that he is avoiding it. In the future, he may avoid similar obstacles whether they are on line or not.

Let's suppose that you are sending your dog on a mark that involves his going directly through a small body of water, 20' across, from a distance of 100 yards. The requirements are clear and the mark is obvious, yet when your dog reaches the water he runs around it. Do you burn him the instant he starts to make his cheating move on the run? No. Let the dog commit to the error far enough so that your sit whistle comes as he is abreast of the water, rather than when he is close to the correct water entry.

An admonishment of "No! Sit!" is now in order while the dog is sitting facing you, accompanied with a nick on the collar. Next, whistle your dog back in front of the pond and attempt to cast him, from the sitting position, into the water. If this fails, move up. Make it more obvious, and repeat. Avoid long belabored sessions that exhaust the dog. Settle for minor improvements and you will see daily gains.

In training for directness, extremes and ambiguities should be avoided. I was training years ago with a moderately talented trainer who had a brilliant Labrador bitch. A blind retrieve required her to brush a point of cover jutting out into a field of shorter grass. The session went on for about half an hour. If the dog took the point of cover too deep she got corrected. If she flared the point slightly, she got cor-

Teach your retriever to come back straight, too.

rected. She was put in a can't-win situation in which her trainer degenerated into cussing and whipping her with a belt. The fact that this bitch survived this and doubtless other training mistakes is testimony to her greatness.

Directness of return may seem insignificant by comparison to getting there on a straight line. Don't be fooled. Many dogs have been taught to go out straight followed by relaxed standards on the returns. We have been guilty of this. FC Banjo, who was naturally a straight-line dog on land and water, frequently returned by time-consuming, deviated paths. In retrospect, we realize because she required minimal correction to go straight to the bird, her training did not include a proper return. A talented marker, Banjo could fail a test when the indirection of her return led to her forgetting where she had been.

With most dogs, who need a modicum of corrective training to go straight, ignoring the return route will lead to failings in directness going out. If high standards are maintained throughout, going and coming, notions of skirting obstacles will gradually lessen. The simple act of moving down shore as you call the returning dog, making the water route more obvious, helps to establish honesty going and coming. Repeating "Here!" every time your dog turns his head toward the cheating route helps keep him coming straight (make it loud!). Once the cheating habit is established, however, dogs tend not to respond to this tactic. Again, as we've mentioned before, be moderate in your demands. Don't make overly difficult obstacle courses of your training sessions, and avoid ambiguity.

Handling to instill straight returns uses the same principles

Move down shore to influence a dog to stay in the water on the return.

and reinforcements that are employed in establishing directness going out.

The rope possibly has less application on the return than do hazing and handling accompanied by the e-collar. This is owing to the problem that very long check cords are cumbersome to handle. Also, it is inadvisable to haul your dog too vigorously with the check cord. On land this activity creates resistance, and in the water too much pulling leads to panic and possibly drowning of the dog. The main purpose of the check cord is to make the dog feel "under wraps" and to remind him of the direction he must take.

As we have stated, dogs with established cheating habits do not respond to all of these methods as well as young, inexperienced trainees. Once a dog is convinced "Back" means "get there however you like" and "Here" means "take any route so long as you end up here," instead of "come straight toward me," he is going to have a hard time understanding that you want to dictate his route. With an inveterate cheater, we recommend handling. Give him only marks with no possibility of cheating while you teach him to handle.

With most dogs, attrition will work. Gradually they come to recognize that the seemingly-easy route leads to nothing but sit-whistles. Be patient, as dogs can have a hard time recognizing that an obstacle, once avoided, might be a viable route. We have seen good, straight-line dogs struggle to understand that they should cross a pothole of water, having just once run around it. It is proportionately harder for the dog who has the mindset of thinking "never go through." As straightforward as it is to us, remember that no amount of training on what doesn't work (running around) can tell the dog what does work (going through). Use the minimum of heat required to keep your retriever under control as he struggles with this puzzle—and keep your setups as simple as possible, with obvious destinations.

Once your dog makes the breakthrough and takes the water, keep practicing straightforward tests using attrition until it registers that going straight is a lot less hassle.

Dogs with extremely weak motivation and a wimpy attitude toward water and cover may never get this.

Some retrievers have the opposite problem—too much emphasis on staying in the water has left them fearful of getting out on line to the mark. We have seen dogs line up for memory birds with certainty, take a good line, but instead of landing on line, either swim on, parallel to shore, or mill around in the water near the shore, give up, and return to the handler. Such dogs need to learn that leaving the water on line to the destination will lead to success and not punishment. Since they are reluctant to do the right thing, initial setups must be extremely obvious. Throw a single white dummy on the mowed bank of a narrow channel, and send your dog quickly. Once he gets this, you can gradually increase the length of swims, move the bird or dummy farther up the shore, make the mark a memory bird, and so on. Until the lesson is thoroughly in the past, however, be sure you set up tests in which he will not commit other infractions you need to correct—for fear he will misunderstand and think getting out of the water is wrong.

When training FC Penney's Nifty Bouncer—Mitch—I (John) could not get him to come back by water from the opposite shore. I used a check cord and had a long and difficult session that ended in his coming directly back by water. Mitch was a dog with immense drive. It enabled him to accept

This Lab goes straight past the point....

...and returns by the same route.

high levels of force without folding up. Most dogs, however, are not in his category and must be treated differently.

A further note on Mitch is in order. Old habits die hard, as they say. While running Mitch in a Qualifying stake in which he had a substantial lead, the return route on the final duck took him down shore and past a thicket of blackberry briars. It was early spring and the leaves were not out yet, so the thicket didn't look forbidding to the dog. He decided to beach early, which he had been taught not to do, and got so clogged in the briars that he abandoned his bird in order to get through the tangle. Honesty going and coming can keep your dog out of trouble. That might be its main purpose.

JAFFER'S BLACKIE

by John

FC/AFC JAFFER'S BLACKIE was not only a dog with unusual talent and drive, but an interesting trainee in many ways. Directness was an area in which he excelled. He was a strong and direct water dog with equal abilities on land.

Like most dogs, Blackie needed reminders under certain circumstances to maintain the line he was taking without fudging at the last moment. Recently a friend, also a professional trainer and field trialer, remarked that he had never seen anything so uncanny as Blackie's ability to take long acute angles down shorelines, and at the last moment hit the water on a straight line. The question came up—how did I train him to do that?

When dogs demonstrate an ability to absorb sophisticated lessons, the method of teaching is hard to describe. Similar techniques are unlikely to work on most other dogs.

An analysis of this piece of training with Blackie would suggest an unlikely chance for success. You aim your dog at the water, and correct him for cheating the shore. The result? Most likely, the next send he gets in early.

In Blackie's case, his being a bold water dog, I employed the e-collar in a way that I would not recommend today. I sent Blackie down the shoreline. When he reached the proper place to enter the water, perhaps 100 yards distant, I hit him with the collar and hollered "Back!" while he was on the run. The result was magnificent. He learned to take long angled lines to the water and then enter with a spectacular splash at the ideal moment.

Today I recommend stopping the dog at that ideal point and casting into the water. Insist that he take the cast. At the same time, I work on overly squared (early) entries on long lines into the water. If you have a bright dog with lots of drive, he will get it.

I disclaim accountability for the progress of your dog if you try to do it as I did with Blackie. Happy accidents are rare, but the woods are full of unhappy ones.

CHAPTER 8

SUFFICIENT RANGE

A HUNTING DOG'S NATURAL range determines much of his potential. If he can't make it to his objective, he can't return with the bird.

Many dogs show excellent range from puppyhood on. It is an inherited trait, related to a dog's courage, keen eyesight, athletic ability, and desire to get the game. Dogs with substantial range, despite its obvious value, pose certain obstacles that need to be overcome in training.

The tendency to disappear "over the hill" can be a problem with some wide rangers. We have found that our best field trial bitches have been inclined to escape our control, hunting on their own sometimes for hours. Willfulness, and an inclination to turn off commands at long distance, are also constant challenges with wide rangers.

Make sure retrievers who show no hesitancy to carry long distance are under control on the "Sit" and "Here" commands at all times. We trained a yellow Lab a few years ago who made

Master Hunter easily and also had some success in field trials. He didn't stop on the whistle on blinds, though, beyond 150 yards. Occasionally I got him through a tough set of blinds with luck, but you don't get lucky often in this game. Whether his failure to stop on the whistle was due to a hearing defect, or some other cause, I don't know, but it probably cost him his field championship. His marking and lining were superb, but that is not enough.

Dogs with inadequate range are another matter. At the extreme level, they seem reluctant to get far from their handler. Most hunt short on marks, and are difficult to cast back on blinds. They tend to waffle from side to side, hunting prematurely, or break down and quit.

There are a variety of reasons for this limitation. First, some dogs are born without much ambition. They'd rather hang around your feet. Lazy is the word. Second, vision may be a problem. Long distance vision is required to focus on distant falls enabling them to carry to the area of the bird. Third, training consistently on short marks and blinds will teach the dog to depend on finding the bird at the usual range.

The first two factors, poor natural range and defective vision, respond poorly to remedial efforts. Some improvement can be seen in almost any shortcoming, however, with intelligent training.

Gradual increases in distance coupled to confidence building should improve most cases. Increased visibility of throws and loud shotgun reports help as well. Challenging the lazy or

Visibility and noise from the throwing station help dogs carry to the area of the mark.

the nearsighted dog with concealed throws or barely-audible "Hey! Hey!" shouts before the throw is not going to help.

If your dog hangs up short on marks try forcing him back. Put a little fire under him with the e-collar and a good strong "Back" command after you have his attention. If he is not fully forced on "Back," doing so may help his range, his hunt, and his willingness to take obstacles. Our forcing program uses the stick fetch, followed by forcing to a pile with a stick, forcing to a pile using e-collar pressure behind the sending line, forcing en route with the e-collar, and repetition of the stick and collar force in water—down channels and into or across open water. Progress is measured by the dog's response to the pressure. With most dogs, each new form of pressure will initially be a distraction. Retrieves must be kept short and simple until the dog clearly responds to the force with added impetus to go. If the dog is struggling to get away while we restrain him with a short cord, good. Having to re-steady him later is a small price to pay for a thoroughly forced dog. Once the right response to pressure is established, increase the distance and difficulty of retrieves gradually so as to maintain this response and avoid refusals.

Sometimes lack of range is a result of a dog's lack of familiarity with a new setting. Overall ability to carry the required distances will improve if training sites are varied frequently. Many dogs perform well at long distances on their home turf, but are cautious about venturing far in strange places. We trained a nice Labrador bitch years ago who, owing to circumstances, couldn't be taken to a sufficient variety of training grounds. She trained like a winner at home, but fell apart when taken to field trials.

Factors such as headwinds, cover, and difficult terrain all work against the tendency to carry. Work on developing range first under favorable conditions, and gradually build up versatility by addressing each challenge separately, before combining them.

Something as simple as sore feet can be the problem. Dogs who are left to pace on the concrete in their runs often wear their pads thin. While they show plenty of energy racing back and forth in their kennel, they often won't run in the field. Crating sore-footed retrievers for a spell will usually solve this problem.

More serious health considerations include hip and elbow arthritis, respiratory and heart problems, and blood problems such as anemia. If you suspect health is the reason for your dog's lack of range, a trip to your vet may be necessary.

What is sufficient range? A practical definition is the distance within which almost all game falls, or, in the case of field trials, as far as the human eye can see a bird fall. Distance in field trial tests may seem absurd, and occasionally there are instances where the dog cannot see the thrown bird, or the handler cannot see the dog clearly to handle.

There is no predicting how far a bird may fall from your shooting station. Falls hundreds of yards from the duck blind are common. Yardages can be extreme on pheasant drives in wide open western fields, also. No damage is done by devoting a portion of your training time to working your dog to the limit of its range. We have not observed that dogs trained well on long stuff give up anything on short-range marks and blinds. On the contrary, they seem to do better work at all ranges.

Some time ago, when John was training Dual/AFC Warpath Macho, it became evident that Macho would consistently run past short falls in order to get the long ones. While Macho was not what you would call a fast dog, he was a hustler with good range, and liked to pick up the long birds first. With most dogs, this practice leads to missing the short birds on the next send, as they are disinclined to stop and hunt an area they have run by. John struggled with the problem for some time, trying to get Macho to take the short bird second in a triple, or even first, by selection. It didn't work and Macho exhibited some confusion in the process. It was not until Macho demonstrated his ability to go long, then come back and drill the short bird at a field trial, winning the Open stake, that John decided to let him have his way. It worked and Macho became deadly in competition on the tricky, so-called "indented" marks.

An old standby in encouraging range is to take retrievers for walks in wide-open spaces. As they explore, their fear of being too far from you decreases. You may even take them out with a wide ranging dog and let them run together. In our years of running coonhounds we found that the excitement of pairing a somewhat fearful youngster with a wide-ranging older dog was often what it took to increase range.

Of course, you must have access to a large tract of land where your dog can run but stay out of trouble. Make sure your dog is absolutely reliable on the "Here" command, so you can turn him loose with confidence he will come when called.

As your dog begins to take to these free-wheeling romps, gradually add some other dimensions such as sitting on the whistle at long ranges, coming partway in, then sitting again, and releasing with "OK." Combining the "Here" and "Sit" commands at long range will help to increase control at distances. When you return to blinds and marks you should see improvement both in range and control.

A dog that will go the required distances and obey your commands is an asset in recovering long, difficult birds. We recall many instances in which these attributes saved a bird, while hunting and in competition.

Dogs are not born with equal talents. Many marginal prospects can improve their range with the proper training.

DIXIE

by Amy

D IXIE IS A YELLOW LAB currently in basic training. When she first came to us, Dixie's owners couldn't demonstrate a retrieve, although they told us she would do it under less distracting circumstances. We began work with Dixie. After a few days' adjustment period, we were unable to get her to do an informal retrieve. We have worked with other dogs who never did a play-retrieve but became good retrievers with training, so we began work on obedience and force-fetching. We had to proceed slowly, as Dixie acted fearful and lacked confidence. She seemed not to "tune in" to training—avoiding eye contact and needing more repetition than most dogs.

When Dixie had been with us for three weeks, we had a Chesapeake come in for training. This youngster had had elbow surgery, and was coming to us after three or four weeks of post-surgical rehab. I spoke with Dixie's owner about this. Dixie had been a dysplastic puppy and had undergone a TPO (triple pelvic osteotomy) procedure. The surgeon had assured Dixie's owners she would be sound, but they had asked me to keep an eye on her for lameness or discomfort. They did not seem confident she was fit enough for training. While talking with the rehab people about the other dog, I asked if the TPO procedure could really make a dysplastic dog sound. Their answer amounted to "yes, but she probably needs rehab." Feeling little the wiser, I passed the information on to Dixie's owner, who decided to have the rehab specialists evaluate Dixie.

Dixie spent a month in rehab, after which her owners brought her back to us. They said at the end of her time there that she had seen another dog run a mark and had raised a ruckus. They had tried Dixie on the same mark, and she had done it. They wanted to bring her to one of our field training sessions and show off what she could do.

They got Dixie out of the truck, and I was dumbfounded at the change in her. Although I had noticed a pronounced swing to her gait, I hadn't realized how different her hindquarters looked from those of the other Labs. Seeing her with a well-muscled rear end, I saw the improvement was striking. Her gait was totally different, her hind legs tracking straight with no swing. The changes to her appearance and gait were nothing, however, to the change in her demeanor. She appeared confident and engaged in her surroundings, with only the barest trace of shyness remaining.

I took hold of Dixie's check cord. She responded with eye contact and a brief wag, and heeled with me to the line. I called for the mark, and released her as it fell. She charged out, kept rolling the hundred yards or so to the mark, put on a brief hunt, and returned. Had I not been familiar with her, I would never have believed this was only the second mark she had done in her life. She performed just as well on the other two marks we had set up. The next day Dixie marked at almost twice that distance, hunting short only briefly before working her way back to the mark.

We continued field work for a couple of weeks before returning to force fetching. Dixie demonstrated that her first couple of days' good work was no fluke. Day after day, she marked accurately, showing range, focus, and some ability to hunt when she did not land on the bird exactly.

We have no way of knowing whether Dixie suffered pain, or instability, or just lack of running ability owing to poor muscle tone when she first came to us. We do know that when she was boosted to a level of physical fitness typical of a healthy young Lab, she started to act like a typical healthy young Lab. Her case reminds us that when a dog lacks confidence, willingness, or range, a physical problem may be the cause.

CHAPTER 9

POPPING

P opping—stopping to look at the handler for help when no whistle has been blown—will occur in the training lives of most retrievers. In its infancy, during the early phases of teaching blind retrieves, it is usually a sign of compliance. Later in training it can become a chronic nuisance marring the smoothness of most blinds, and often marks as well. Usually, given fair and consistent training, dogs will pop less frequently as they increase their skill and confidence, until finally the pops disappear altogether. As in other forms of training, a sound foundation will go a long way in preventing problems later in life. With regard to pops, this means an unhurried approach to forcing on back and positive whistle stops.

Before addressing the problem of pops in dogs who are well along in their training, let's examine some of the factors that can create popping in the first place. A breakdown in confidence heads the list.

All retriever training is based on the principle that learning to do the job with confidence, as the trainer has planned it, replaces uncertainty. The trained dog is not an automaton, but the parameters of his work, such as go when sent, go where sent, take obstacles as they come, carry a straight line, hunt relentlessly, be steady, deliver properly—the whole catalogue—become habitual. Worry about mistakes fades as trained behavior becomes habit and the dog rarely gets corrected. Within these limits are infinite opportunities for demonstrations of initiative and talent.

During training, however, the demands of the tasks are increasingly difficult, often diminishing dogs' belief that they can do anything right. At this point, the pop becomes a security blanket stemming from a fear of making mistakes and getting corrected.

A second form of popping is seen in some hard-driving, fast dogs who have what we call the high-speed pop. It consists of a nervous reaction to tests that the dog does not understand well. It's a pop that isn't preceded by a slow-down, often surprising the handler. As training progresses, however, the circumstances under which the popping is likely will become familiar to the trainer.

The third cause of popping, lack of motivation, is the most difficult to treat. At its worst, this is a matter of laziness. There is really not much you can do to improve such dogs other than continually insist on a reasonable level of performance based on natural abilities. Results will vary, but if performance falls consistently below your expectations for a quality retriever, you may have to consider another dog.

A few dogs, though they appear to have a lot of drive, will begin to appear lackluster if the workload becomes too demanding. FC Banjo XXXVI was a one- or at most two-test per day dog. Her progress was at its best when we trained her on just one hard set-up per day. More than that, and her effectiveness would decline, giving rise to pops.

When confusion is the primary cause, pops can be at least

Pressure behind the line helps clarify the requirement: Get the bird.

partially treated by clarifying the test. Reducing the multiple marks to singles, moving the line up on difficult or ambiguous water entries, or taking the heat off and teaching by repetition are approaches that may work. Even though these measures are worth taking, the pop itself is probably going to need some specific attention.

One of the first dogs to make Field Champion while in our training program was a bitch named Penney of Evergreen. When John got her in training she was about nine years old and had a history of popping on water blinds. The problem was so severe that she couldn't buy a place in the Open. Penney was not trained on the e-collar by her two previous trainers, and John was doubtful that it would apply well at this stage in her life. John's technique consisted of sending her on a blind, then running as closely as he could behind her so that when the pop occurred, he could begin his noisy admonishments: "Get back, damn your hide, get back!" Penney took this to heart, and it wasn't long before the pop disappeared and she was winning trials.

In the '60s John trained his dog Tar who popped at the water's edge. Tar didn't want to get wet, from the time he was a puppy. John followed Tar as closely as possible, caught him when he popped, and gave him two or three whacks on the rump with a training stick while repeating "Back, back, back!" This worked on Tar as well as on a golden named Sport who would go ten yards on the memory bird of a double, then pop. John counted the days that he ran out to Sport to correct him with the stick and the "Back" command. It was thirty. On the thirtieth day Sport took off when sent on the memory bird, slowed down at his usual popping point, but didn't pop. John sold Sport to another trainer, but so long as he had him, the pop never recurred.

We have used the technique of running after the dog with a training stick during force-to-pile and early forcing on "Back." It seems to be readily comprehended by many dogs, and can be used to get them past occasional hang-ups in the field.

Trying to eliminate pops can be an elusive and frustrating experience for trainer and dog. The advent of the electric collar, however, raised the level of success in treating this malady. With improvements in reliability and adjustability of shock strength, e-collars have become an increasingly effective tool.

Treating popping in the field without backing up for remedial work is a temptation, but usually isn't conducive to progress. If your dog is already well trained and for some reason begins to pop on blinds, or marks, perhaps corrections in the field will do the trick. Even with seasoned veterans, however, resorting to a carefully conceived drill may produce better and more lasting results.

We dislike shocking dogs on the run. There's too much chance of the dog's misinterpreting the correction. Instead we get the dog under control in a sitting position facing the handler. We then give a short sit blast on the whistle, momentary shock, then repeat "Sit." The dog is now under control. Let

Establish forcing on a back cast as a drill before using it in the field.

him sit for a while, then raise a hand, command, "Back," momentary shock, and repeat "Back!" while the dog is in motion. When it can be seen that this maneuver is working, the dog has demonstrated an understanding of enforcement for "Sit" and "Back." This is crucial to the elimination of pops. Of course the seasoned performer who has already had this training will usually respond as if all he needed was a refresher. Those who have never had the "stop and go" basics solidly applied need to learn these fundamentals. Suspending work on marks may help your retriever to focus on this lesson.

Similarly, for the dog that has been trained to go when sent, a simple, drill-like setup will help make the requirements clear. A channel of water 20' wide or so, and 75 to 100 yards in length is a good training site. After establishing a straight line up the channel, introduce "pressure en route" in the form of a repeat of the "Back!" command and a nick with the collar. Strive for results without wearing it into the ground. An eager dog can handle this without getting down.

Pops on marks, and pops on blinds, land or water, frequently call for different treatments. The reason is clear. Pops on marks usually have to do with fear of mistakes, such as switching or returning to old marks, both of which they have been rigorously taught not to do. Marks that are excessively tight, either with birds falling close to one another, particularly at longer distances, or a narrow angle between the lines to the marks, may confuse the dog as to which retrieve he can make without correction. Lighten up the test and continue to remind your dog that the pop is not acceptable.

Fear of overrunning marks may cause popping. If the mark is close, and retired, a distant flier down last may erase the short bird from your dog's memory. Hammering him with whistle stops and shock, then handling to the short, forgotten bird is almost sure to create pops. Here the popping needs less attention than the necessity to reduce the marking combinations to an understandable level.

If your dog is popping on the long retired mark, then your problem is similar to the case in which he will not carry sufficiently on a long blind. The treatment is like the previously described "Sit, Back!" drill.

Dogs will often pop on water blinds in which they are sent

*Train to promote
clarity and confidence.*

on lines, or commanded to take a cast, resembling a situation
that they have been taught to avoid. Such things as getting out
of the water early on a long swim, or crossing a point when the
safe thing appears to be swimming around, can provoke popping. This response is similar to an inexperienced dog's confusion when cast where it doesn't want to go. His choice of route
results in an immediate whistle; the dog has been shown what
won't work, but doesn't know what will. To lessen your dog's
anxiety, train for success on the cast followed by success on the

blind, keeping correction minimal. An excellent performer will go wherever sent and cast into obstacles without hesitation or popping. Stop the dog, use light momentary shock, repeat "Back" with the appropriate cast, and the pops should soon be replaced with compliance.

Bear in mind that popping is not malicious, nor does it prove your dog is no good. Usually, it indicates a failure in basic training followed by tests that are beyond his comprehension. Taking care that the bases are thoroughly covered in early training will help to ensure that popping, when it occurs, can be treated effectively before it becomes a chronic problem.

PUDGE

"**P**UDGE," FC OAKHILL EXPONENT, was a very fast, aggressive Labrador bitch. Despite her drive, she was a born popper. It had nothing to do with training to stop on the whistle, as I didn't start that until she was nearly three. She would line spectacularly at one and a half years of age and was an excellent marker as well. But her work was flawed by the recurrent pop.

Since nothing in particular seemed to cause the pop, I was at a loss for something to remove to correct the problem. I felt like the woman in the story told by Mark Twain. She was very ill and was advised by her doctor to give up smoking, drinking, and swearing. When she protested that she did none of these things, the doctor responded, "You're a sinking ship with no freight to throw overboard."

Months went by in Pudge's training with no change in the frequency of popping. At about a year and a half of age I put her through two consecutive months of forcing on "Back," 30 days on land and 30 days in the water. I repeated the training when she was just under three. Seems like a lot, doesn't it? But that's what it took. Still, the pop persisted in, of all areas, land marks. If there were two sets of guns far out in the field, Pudge would almost always pop before getting to the area of either mark.

I was stymied, for the time, and actually quite discouraged with Pudge's prospects as a field-trial dog. Since Pudge had been thoroughly forced on back twice in her life with the stick and the collar, I decided to address the problem in the field. When the pop occurred, I'd get on the button. Hot, at that time, was the only strength. I hollered "Back!" I didn't require a stop and sit as we now recommend. It worked the first time I tried it and with two or three more applications the problem appeared cured. Of course, in dogs like Pudge (a born popper), it reappeared from time to time, but rarely.

I recall Pudge's first Open win in which she ran flawlessly, except for two pops fairly well out on a water blind. Each of these pops occurred immediately following a shotgun blast from a nearby stake, but I was still disappointed. I said to the judge upon leaving the line, "Sorry about those pops." His reply was, "Oh, we expect to see a pop when a gun goes off like that, close by." Gratefully, I left the line, put Pudge in the truck, and returned later to ace the water triple. I knew in my heart, though, that Pudge might have been saved by those gunshots. She might have popped without them.

CHAPTER 10

BLINKING BIRDS AND BUGGING

B LINKING, OR DELIBERATELY avoiding downed game, is a fault that renders retrievers useless. If your prospect did not show adequate bird interest when you embarked upon his training, you probably would have sought another dog. We assume, then, that the problem was created.

What can you do to a dog that will prevent him from wanting the bird? Lots of things. Let's begin with force-fetching. If your dog is a particularly tough assignment at this stage, you might introduce birds too soon. We try to prevent souring during force-fetching, especially where birds are concerned. For this reason we force fetch on objects other than birds, such as dummies or wooden dowels. Done correctly, of course, the force-fetch training will increase enthusiasm for whatever objects you are using.

Premature exposure to hunting conditions can also cause blinking. Suppose you knock down a cripple and your dog takes a beating from the wings of a strong goose or a scratch from the spurs of a cock pheasant, causing lasting fear. The need to introduce your youngster to live birds in training is obvious.

During her training, FC Oakhill Exponent frequently made retrieves through live game, mostly geese, on some training ponds. As a result, birdy as she was, she ignored shackled ducks when first introduced to them. She must have thought they were local wild birds not to be retrieved. A little work with shackled ducks solved the problem and she quickly learned to pick up crippled ducks in hunting and field-trial situations.

Some of the things we must teach our retrievers for competition may cause blinking. The "poisoned bird" test is an example. If this test is taught incorrectly, that is, if direct collar pressure is used to discourage the dog from picking up the "poison" bird, blinking may result. A foundation in handling should be adequate to ensure successful handling away from a tempting bird before this test is introduced. If your dog's handling is hazy, and he is in the act of picking up the poison bird when you nick him with the collar, you may break him not only from picking up that bird, but also others. FC Banjo XXXVI was so susceptible to this kind of training that a mere command of "No" before sending her past a poison bird would cause her not only to avoid the bird on the initial send, but also to blink it when sent to pick it up. We never solved the problem, but we were guaranteed that she wouldn't pick up the poison bird if we said "No bird."

Some field-trial judges have carried poison-bird and associated tests to unreasonable extremes. We have seen pheasants placed directly on line to a blind retrieve. Another test that bears mention consists of a shot bird as part of a multiple mark. The shot bird is picked up by the gunners while the contestant retrieves another. You are then required to send your dog for the picked-up bird, allow him to establish a hunt, and then on the judges' OK, handle your dog to a blind in another area. We think it is unnecessary to confront dogs in field trials or hunt tests with such confusion, and we are sure that if we train on such stuff we can create blinking.

Excessive heat and grinding on marking tests can cause blinking. Frequently a dog who has encountered too much failure in marking will appear to give up, showing little interest in finding game. Dogs in this state are apt to take another unwanted step by intentionally steering clear of the fall.

Occasionally dogs will blink birds for reasons other than an accumulation of training errors. Lack of familiarity with the game to be retrieved can be a factor. We have participated in hunt tests in which chukar partridges were used. Several dogs that retrieved other species well blinked the chukars, perhaps because of unfamiliarity. We have had dogs that blinked doves on their first dove hunt. Pudge, FC Oakhill Exponent, when sent from the boat on her first Canada goose, showed surprise when she got to the twelve-pound bird, but retrieved it flawlessly.

Dogs (males, that is) will frequently blink a bird if sent to an area in which bitches (females, that is) in heat have been working. Testosterone takes over and bird interest disappears. We make a practice of periodic training with dogs on ground on which bitches in heat have been worked. You don't need to make a steady practice of this, for fear of creating other difficulties. Our method employs the e-collar. When the dog puts his nose down to enjoy bitch scent, we say "No, Here!" accompanied by a nick with the collar. Then we move to the bird and command "Fetch," perhaps with an accompanying ear pinch or collar nick if he has been forced with the collar. Usually a few repetitions will serve to ensure your dog's retrieve, even though he encounters heat scent along the way.

In cases in which the training off bitch scent requires considerable pressure, you will likely find that your dog will refuse to breed. This is an issue that can usually be resolved with expert handling. Some dogs will only breed in a specific setting, such as the back yard. But this is preferable to having your dog yield to the "call of the wild" when there are birds to be retrieved.

Probably the most common reason for bird blinking is "burnout." Dogs, just like people, have a breaking point, and it is our business as trainers to avoid passing that point. D. L. Walters once made the comment that it was his opinion that most amateurs train too much. There is much to be said for quitting before exhaustion begins to affect dog or trainer. Most pros, owing to their number of trainees, do not over-train. Short, to-the-point sessions with regular frequency are the answer, not long, belabored harangues.

Blinking, in general, can be treated by first removing the

cause. Whether it is a result of overwork, confusing training, or other mistakes, remove it. Add more bird work to your dog's training. Shot fliers and lots of work with birds he especially likes are good. Be sure to give your dog an abundance of the birds you are likely to encounter while hunting or in formal events. Of course, if you're invited to a sandhill crane hunt, you'll simply have to rely on luck.

Bugging

"Bugging" refers to a retriever's intentional avoidance of focusing on marks being thrown, or the attempts of his handler to give a line on a blind or marked retrieve. It becomes almost impossible to do a mark well or achieve a decent line on a blind when your dog bugs. Why do they do it? You would

This Lab's body is lined up correctly, but she looks away.

think a dog born with sufficient talent and drive would always want to get the bird, yes? Not necessarily.

Many factors can interrupt a retriever's eagerness to get the game. To enumerate a few: too many complicated tests; ambiguity (what is right, or wrong); too much training pressure, contradictory corrections, etc. When the load of unpleasant experiences in the training program overbalances a dog's natural enthusiasm for work, the result is natural—avoidance.

Bugging can be a particularly difficult problem to address because, while added force is seen by many as the cure, physical correction is often what got the dog down to begin with. On the other hand, if you remove most physical correction your dog may conclude that bugging is a good way to avoid pressure. The same goes for simplifying your demands on difficult tests, although this is generally a better choice than dramatically reducing pressure. In the course of training, you want to see continual gains in skill, with a minimum of backtracking. If you have overreached, yes, it is necessary to fill in the missing steps. Retreating unnecessarily, however, or too far, can harm your ability to keep a dog moving forward. Dogs' tolerance for learning, for attempting the unfamiliar, needs to be maintained. Thus it is desirable, in treating bugging, to identify the aspect of training that has caused the problem, instead of resorting to blanket simplification.

Obviously, if you construct a training program that is full of contradictions, your dog will be confused. For this reason, it is necessary to teach each lesson so the demands are clear.

When contradictions inevitably come up, trainees must understand that, "Yes, you did it that way yesterday, but today I want you to do it another way." Bright dogs are quick to comprehend distinctions regarding the permissibility of certain actions under various conditions. Of course, if your dog isn't bright that's a problem.

Is there an encompassing principle for the treatment of bugging? Perhaps. Is there a sure cure once it is firmly entrenched? Probably not. A wise initial choice when a dog bugs is to remove him from the working environment that created it. If he's bugging on marks only, as some dogs will, remove marking temporarily. If he bugs on lining up for

Sometimes dogs mark better, and don't bug, when the handler steps back and leaves them to it.

blinds, stop lining. A solution might be to do all blinds for a while from a remote casting position; that is, take your dog into the field, make him sit, return to the line, and give him a cast to begin the blind.

With bugging on marks, we have had good results by taking the retriever to the line and backing off a few steps, allowing him to mark without interference from the handler.

If you choose to treat the behavior by suspending a phase of his work (marks, blinds, or both), what comes next? Probably obedience drills, coupled to some relaxation resulting from his vacation from the daily grind. Heeling, sitting, and here/sit drills will sharpen his responses and may have the effect of reducing bugging.

There is also the frontal approach, the one used by most trainers of our acquaintance, but it's not always the most effective. As your dog begins bugging while sitting at your side, step briskly forward with the command "Heel," followed by a nick from the e-collar or a tap on the back with the training stick. If bugging continues, repeat until he complies by paying attention to the mark, or your efforts to line. Try this for several training sessions, but focus your attention on the bugging rather than on other aspects of the test.

Bugging on blind retrieves may be improved by having a helper throw a bird from a hidden location in line with the direction you are trying to give. The dog may develop the expectation that something good will happen in the direction you are pointing out.

We have noticed among trainers who have a rather high frequency of dogs that bug, that their requirements for a specific line are often excessive. The pattern generally consists of many efforts to line the dog up perfectly, repeated sits and re-heels, much fidgeting over the dog's head with the sending hand, and so forth. Settle for a less precise line, send the dog more quickly, and encourage his efforts with praise.

One other aspect of bugging is worth bringing up. Although uncommon, it occurs with sufficient frequency to warrant mentioning. This is the dog that bugs severely, but only on a limited aspect of his work. An example is due here.

Jade was a talented Lab bitch who was weak in the water in training and competition. John emphasized water work with her to the extent that she became perhaps the best on water blinds he has trained. On water marks, however, she bugged. This failing caused John many disappointments as she got to the final series of the Open only to fail the last bird of the water triple. Jade could mark and she would go where she was sent, but she wouldn't look at the key birds in a water marking test. In retrospect, John feels certain she could have had more success in field trials if water marks had been eliminated from her training.

REAL DOGS

MOLLY

by Amy

MOLLY GOT OFF TO A slow start in training. She had been with another trainer, and had reportedly been force-fetched and introduced to handling, beginning at an earlier age than we would recommend. Her owner felt her training had gone sour. We found Molly would fetch off the ground on command, once per session. After a single fetch, she ignored further commands.

Molly did not deliver to hand reliably, and had a panicky response to correction that disrupted training sessions. We have seen this pattern in other dogs. We think force-fetching early, too quickly, or with too much reliance on pressure as the solution to all hang-ups is the probable cause. We guess that the dog fails to understand the relationship between its actions and our reactions. With Molly, we felt the best thing to do was to take her through the force-fetch sequence ourselves, giving her time to learn that the consequences to her actions are predictable and she can control pressure.

In time, Molly learned to fetch reliably, and acted more stable and confident. She was a good singles marker and picked up lining and casting readily. We encouraged her owners in their expectation that she could run the Senior Hunter. When we started double marks, however, we got a surprise. Molly had a lot of trouble with memory birds. We lightened up on Molly's handling work and concentrated on developing her doubles marking, using singles from multiple gun stations in combination, simple "confidence builder" doubles, schooled doubles, and so forth. Her progress was slow.

We had a cold winter and thought not to subject Molly to long swims, since we didn't want to discourage her. As the weather warmed up, we did more work in the water, and got a surprise: Molly's accuracy and confidence were much greater on water marks than on land marks. We seized this new tool, working on water doubles until she was proficient. After that, her land marking came around much faster. We started running more blinds. Molly handled responsively and proved to be a natural lining dog, readily taking difficult lines with multiple water entries. We were enthusiastic about Molly. She was talented, stylish, hard-going, strong and tough in the water, went straight, and had a wonderful temperament and response to training.

Although Molly was now ready to run the Senior Hunter, her owners left her with us for additional training. We began work on triple marks. I had been handling Molly, but now John began to handle her some of the time. One day he allowed her to run around a pothole of water on her way to the middle mark of a triple. Sometimes we allow an infraction of this kind, then repeat the test insisting on a proper line. Ordinarily it works, and we don't lose ground on the "go straight" principle. In this case, however, it was a flop. Having once run around the water, Molly seemed to have dismissed it as a possible route. John tried and tried to cast her into the water, but Molly responded to every cast by trying to run around to the right or to the left.

Because Molly had always gone straight for me, and been such an eager water dog, I thought perhaps I could get her through the pothole. After giving her a rest, I got her out and tried to run the mark as a single. After many casts and many attempts to run around, I finally got Molly into the water. She went on and picked up the mark. I ran her on it at least one more time, getting her into the water with less resistance.

I don't think we used much if any e-collar pressure on Molly during these sessions. She was clearly confused and, after many failed casts, she stopped trying and I gave her a few smacks on the rear with the training stick to get her going.

In subsequent training sessions we again had trouble with the middle mark of a triple. Molly would try to avoid the water, or try to avoid the middle mark altogether, going back to an old fall. We set simpler triples for Molly, and when the problem persisted, started running singles and doubles with three guns out. Sometimes we ran a test as singles one day, and returned to do the same marks as a triple the next day.

Molly has improved. She is now running "cold" triples competently, but with one hitch. She consistently chooses to leave the middle mark for last, and will not look at it on the send. She looks a little left, a little right, then back to the left, but never locks onto it as she does the left and right marks.

When sent, she goes straight to the mark and almost always gets it without difficulty.

Molly's bugging tendency has spilled over to her blinds. She has become difficult to line up. For fear that excessive fussing over the line may make the problem worse, I usually send her after a moderate effort, thinking to correct a faulty line by handling. Correction is rarely necessary. Molly apparently figures out where I want her to go, and lines accurately, even though she is reluctant to look at the destination when I try to line her up.

We don't know if Molly's problem originated with that first session involving a struggle on the middle bird, or if this is a reprise of the difficulty she had learning doubles. We do believe that the solution fits with our usual approach of simplifying the tasks the dog is asked to do, and working to build confidence. The trend is in the right direction. Molly no longer tries to avoid doing the middle mark, or to avoid obstacles on the way, and she retrieves it with good style. We think it important, though, to keep trying to build confidence until she is lining up properly.

CHAPTER 11

MARKING PROBLEMS

I T HAS BEEN SAID, by experienced field trialers, that the most difficult thing to teach a retriever is marking on land. It is not hard to see why.

Most good retrievers are fast. Speed enables dogs to get to their objectives in the shortest possible time. It also makes it easy for dogs to overrun short birds en route to longer ones, to switch from one bird to another when the falls are close together ("tight"), and to make other mistakes that lead to memory failure. Confusion in marking on land can just as easily occur in hunting situations in which multiple falls land so close together that a legitimate area of hunt overlaps that of another bird. Retrievers may retrieve a bird without a clear idea of which one they have picked up.

In hunting settings, the problem of dealing with these overly tight birds is clear—send the dog for the other bird, and if necessary, handle. In field trials, however, handling on marks is usually the kiss of death. Good judges avoid excessively tight marks in order to present contestants with reasonable marking challenges, as opposed to tests that are nearly impossible for dogs to decipher.

The principle of clarity should be followed throughout marking training, particularly with individuals who show little natural talent. Those dogs who are unusually gifted with marking and memory abilities frequently reveal this early in life and go on to be substantially faster learners and higher achievers than others.

Puppies should be given a healthy dose of marking practice before they have received much other formal training. If they can be steadied by restraint, induced to pick up the bird or dummy on natural instinct, and taught to return directly when

Restraining a puppy as she watches a mark.

called, marking practice is of benefit at an early age. Many of our puppies retrieve at three to four months of age. Force fetching and basic training are still a couple of months in the future. If you have a prospect that is a complete renegade and will never return with the dummy or bird, postpone marking until he is through force fetching.

An early start on easy retrieves builds confidence. The puppy who believes he can mark and recover anything is on the right track. Don't do anything to impair his confidence.

Developing marking skill in adults follows the same principles we apply to puppies. Simplicity, clarity, and consistency of demands are paramount.

The spectator at an All-Age field trial event, or a Master level hunt test, may be tempted to think that, since these are the things retrievers are required to do, he should go home and practice them. Highly sophisticated marking tests are not taught by practicing them as you see them in formal events, however.

Marking combinations (doubles, triples, and quadruples) are taught by working on singles with multiple throwers in the field, or through the use of walking singles in which a helper moves from place to place in the field while throwing a number of different marks.

By this method dogs are taught to concentrate on one mark at a time, not to ramble around the field looking for results in odd places. Concentration on individual marks (singles) is the key to precise marking.

Top competitors are maintained, not trained in early life, by frequent exposure to field-trial level marking tests. At some point, even these wizards will be seen to stumble. At this point, the wise trainer will generally break the three- or four-bird test down into doubles or singles in order to make things more comprehensible to the dog who is having trouble.

There are many tools that trainers may employ to enhance marking skills. Some of these are unique to training on marks, but many have overlapping benefits for other areas as well.

Retrievers are birdy. They love birds and are excited and energized by them. If not, they are probably not worth the training that goes into them. This love of birds can often be converted into marking excellence. The shot flier is the high point in most retrievers' lives. It's what they live for and what they anticipate.

Shot fliers usually improve marking.

Shooting fliers, pigeons, ducks, and pheasants, particularly at the longer distances, will measurably increase marking skills in almost any retriever. We think it would require a huge expense in shot birds to overdo this aspect of training. Of course, there are some downsides to fliers. Some dogs will become increasingly excited and unsteady with too many fliers, and frequent exposure to cripples can lead to mouth problems.

Multiple marks with fliers can create head-swinging. The flier is often the breaking bird and is down last. To remedy this problem, place the flier in the long bird location and shoot it first, followed by the closer birds.

Dead birds can also enhance marking. Even though they don't have the same attraction as live birds, retrievers still distinguish them from dummies.

The level of noise accompanying marks can be varied to give marking a boost. If you have been saying "Hey, hey!" then throwing the mark, try the blank pistol, or the shotgun—either a shotgun firing blanks or a shotgun simulator.

While we recognize the benefits of live birds, dead birds, and increased noise levels approximating the shotgun as a means of encouraging marking, there is no substitute for establishing enthusiasm for that drab old retrieving dummy, which is the mainstay of our training equipment.

Retrievers, being so in love with the idea of fetching, can be brought along so as to develop nearly as strong a desire for bumpers as they show for birds. In fact, we feel that something is going wrong with dogs that are not enthusiastic on dummies.

It pays to establish enthusiasm for dummies.

All of our dogs are taught not to scale the sides of our dog trailer in attempt to get dummies that have been put out of reach. We are careful not to leave dummies piled on the ground, particularly when young dogs are being trained, as they can be distracting. We expect to see about the same level of enthusiasm for dummies as we do birds, yet there is an undeniable something that is added by the use of birds, especially shot fliers.

Use a hierarchy of elements of difficulty when training on marking. If your dog is failing to show effectiveness on long distance marks, for example, reduce challenges other than distance to the lowest possible level. Keeping the terrain simple is one method of putting the long mark within the reach of a dog that is having problems. A golf course is ideal. Let him take the fairway.

Use large, very white bumpers thrown against a background of dark trees. Keep the sun at your back. Dogs don't see much better looking into the sun than you do. Have your thrower wear a white jacket. You want your dog to see where the mark is going to come from. Time your blank pistol or shotgun discharge so that it immediately precedes the throw. If the shot is too early (or the throw too late), the dog's attention will drift to another area, and he will not see the throw. If it is obvious to you that your dog has not seen the throw, have it repeated. If he fails to see it a second time, move up or have your helper shout and wave the dummy before shooting and throwing. Try to make it easy for your dog.

When your dog has achieved some skill on marks thrown at various distances, practice multiple marks beginning with doubles built on singles. By this we mean establish a single that your dog can do well, then add a throw that is much closer, perhaps off-line as a second mark or "diversion" as it is sometimes called.

Beware of echoes. In some places they are worse than others. If your shot reverberates, giving a delayed stimulus during the marking test, your dog will more than likely look in the direction of the echo, thereby missing the mark. This problem can be alleviated by timing the shot and the throw simultaneously.

We discussed feeding marks while a dog is en route in Chapter 7, on Directness. This procedure applies to marking as well. Suppose you are working on a particularly difficult mark and your dog is showing signs of breaking down while he is on the way to it. Have your helper supplied with dummies ready to repeat the throw on command. You are trying to keep your dog briefed on the location of the mark, making success easier.

Difficult marks that have significant challenges—such as ditches, water and cover hazards, crossing points or islands requiring a second or third water entry—should be approached as singles. In order to get the most benefit from tests of this type, your dog should have been trained to handle. If the mark is in the water on the far side of a point or an island, make the throw conspicuous, preferably a white dummy he can see on the approach. A visible splash on the throw is helpful. If your dog has trouble with the point or island, either refusing to get on it, which may happen, or staying on it and cheating the shore the rest of the way, handle him through it, reward with a "Good boy," and repeat. Keep the pressure off. You are building confidence, not fear of the test. It would be impractical to enumerate all the possibilities on difficult singles. The key is to vary them and keep your dog's confidence up.

In all aspects of training a balance must be maintained. In marking, if your dog learns to do one arrangement well, an undue emphasis may affect others. A few years back, a friend trained a fine field champion, Chance, who had only one serious flaw. If he had to swim in a channel, he would not get out of the water for a mark partway down the shore. Chance was drilled on staying in the water to the extent that he would swim past marks until he reached the end of the water. More often than not, though, in hunting and in field trials, the dog that stays in the water gets the bird. Dog training is a calculated risk. Those who train rigorously to keep their dogs swimming win more than those who permit bank running.

As we move to multiple and retired marks, problems and pitfalls increase. In these circumstances dogs confront the difficulty of the individual marks, plus the arrangement.

We wrote of adding a short, easy bird to a difficult single, creating a double composed of a hard memory bird and an easy diversion. This usually is a good way to proceed. As you put two throws, more distant, in the field, it is a good idea to practice singles first and repeat later as a double. Your dog should act keyed-in when he faces the double as if to say, "Oh, I've seen this, and I can do it." This method of building tests can be employed with the addition of a third or fourth bird. Avoid obscure throws that are hard for your dog to see, and excessive tightness that creates confusion as to which bird he has picked up.

A trainer of field trial dogs from Minnesota stated that he always started out training on a triple or quadruple by throwing the marks as singles in the order they would be picked up when the test was done as a multiple. Let us explain. The last bird thrown is usually picked up first. The next would be the closer remaining mark, and the last would be the long memory bird. There are many variations on this model, but the singles are thrown in the order they are ordinarily picked up in the triple or quad.

We have succeeded with another approach to teaching dif-

Sending a dog for a mark.

ficult marking combinations. When John was first running the Open stake, he took his cue from the tests in the previous weekend's trial. On Monday, following the trial, he set up an approximation of the test, throwing single marks with dummies. On Tuesday, he repeated the test as a multiple mark using dead birds, and on Wednesday, he set up the same test with a shot flier on one station. Judges at that time, as well as today, tended to fall into modes of certain types of tests and present similar versions of them from week to week. It so happens, in formal events, that if your dog is not prepared to face what is in vogue you will have little success.

What about retired guns? In hunt tests your retriever will be required to mark multiple falls in which nearly all of the gunning stations are obscure. In the advanced level of field trials, one or two of the gunners are apt to retire (hide) after the marks are thrown. An effective way to train for retired guns is to avoid using them too early in your dog's training. First, establish marking as the priority with all guns visible, then in steps introduce the retired thrower. Retire the thrower in the easiest location first, progressing to the more challenging ones as your dog learns. In cases where retired guns pose particular difficulties it may be wise to run the mark with the throwers out, then repeat with the throwers hidden.

The order in which marks are thrown can pose problems in addition to the challenges of each. When we first saw "out of order" fliers in field trials, we were surprised. The normal course of events in the Open consisted of two memory birds, one long, one medium, with the third bird, a shot flier, down

The dog watches a fall to the ground, while handler John looks at the next station.

last. It threw the dogs off to see the flier first or second in a triple. The result was often confusion and failure on the test. Judges have devised ways over the years to keep contestants and their dogs off balance. A good axiom for the advanced field trial dog and gun dog is that he should be able to do anything—within reason. Of course, you must practice!

With regard to unusually difficult marking tests, years ago a double was developed that almost no one could do well. It was often expanded to a triple, but it really didn't need it. The test was dubbed the McAssey indent after its presumed originator. This test consisted of a short dead bird thrown so as to land about midway between the line of sending and the long gunner who shot a live bird second. In some cases the short gunning station retired as the dogs usually went for the flier, although leaving the short gunners out didn't seem to do much to make the test easier. The test was usually set so that the wind would not allow the dogs to catch the scent of the short bird en route to the flier. Selection of the short bird over the flier as the first retrieve made this test fairly easy for some dogs, but judges soon learned to beat the selection gambit by readjusting the arrangement of birds.

The method John used for beating this test was to begin by training on the double in the traditional way—long bird first, short second. Pick up the short bird, then the long—a piece of cake. Then the test was repeated but with the order of throws reversed—short bird first, long bird second. The youngsters, who had just picked them up short first and long second, would do the same when the order was reversed. John was teaching selection in a painless way. FC Oakhill Exponent was midway through marking training at two years or so, and had learned to select in this way. At this point judges learned to set up their tests to penalize the highly trained selecting dogs. Major trainers the country over forsook selection training in favor of "positive marking," which is essentially—get the last bird down first, then remember the others.

Fortunately, "Pudge" was not brainwashed to the extent that selection had become a firm habit. It so turned out that she retained her ability to select when needed, or she could take the marks in an order that was more straightforward. If you plan to run your dog in field trials or hunt tests, you must keep tuned in.

Marking in the water poses an array of problems in addition to those encountered on land. In some set-ups the water is an obstacle on the way to a land mark. When marks fall in the water, special problems arise.

Marks that are thrown on land across a piece of water require repetition until the dog is comfortable with the fact that his momentum has been interrupted by a swim. The requirement here is obvious—practice. In the case of marks that fall in the water, new challenges are added.

One, a retriever's natural inclination to carry to the far side of a body of water and hunt the land can cause him to pass by the mark. Second, marks that fall in the water are harder to find because depth perception while swimming is impeded

The swimming dog's eye level is only inches above the water's surface.

and scenting conditions are poorer than on land. If you get in the water with your eyes at dogs'-eye-level, you will see little of floating objects. This explains why a retriever with good vision can approach, and fail to see, white floating dummies that are clearly visible to the handler from his elevated position. Soggy ducks float low in the water. Often retrievers get within a couple of feet of these birds without finding them if the dog is not in position to wind them.

Marking in the water is improved if the light is good, reflection off the water is minimal, and the dummy or bird makes a visible splash. Then, getting to the area of the fall, where the nose comes into play, is easier. Marking training should be conducted with a high ratio of success, particularly on water marks.

All dogs are not eager in the water. For some, swimming is a chore. Others show more aptitude. Strong water dogs benefit from larger doses of water work than weak ones. Thus, they may profit from more drilling and repetition, or longer swims.

There is a factor known to retriever trainers as "memory leakage." Owing to extra time consumed while swimming, as opposed to running over land, there is a greater tendency for retrievers to forget. In addition, straight lines are a more urgent requirement. Dogs that continually wander off line frequently end up in no man's land or, more accurately, "no bird water."

The principles of teaching marking on land apply to water, but more stringently. Long swims should be taught as singles while making every effort at clarity and success.

Handling is useful to teach retrievers to stay on line in the water. Crosswinds, attractive clumps of cover, points and islands, or scent from previously retrieved birds tend to pull retrievers off line. As training progresses, distractions can be introduced and handling employed to keep the dog on line. Throws should be as obvious as possible so failure to hold the line is a result of succumbing to temptation rather than memory loss.

Practicing water marks in harsh weather is not advisable. Cold water, below about 56 degrees F, makes concentration harder for the dog, just as our ability to concentrate decreases with discomfort. You need to know your dog, however. Some show no diminishment of marking ability in cold water. These dogs are rare. Even dogs who seem extraordinarily resistant to cold will show symptoms of discomfort and disinterest if exposed long enough.

Some trainers practice one water marking test per week for advanced dogs. Water tests are more time-consuming, are harder to set up, and frequently require more travel to find adequate settings. We like to do some water work nearly every day. Marks needn't all be long, nor do they necessarily have to be multiples. Many tests involving a demand for honesty, carrying hazards, or finding birds in difficult locations, can be practiced on short or medium, as well as long retrieves.

If your dog begins to show less enthusiasm for water marks you are probably overdoing them, or perhaps using too much correction while the dog is swimming. Avoid shocking dogs while swimming if possible. If water becomes a generally unpleasant environment for a dog, you can expect him to develop a negative attitude. Enthusiasm for water marks can be boosted, as on land, by increasing the use of birds.

Make water as pleasant and safe a place as it can be. Correction for failures to get wet on the correct line, no-goes, or other such infractions should be administered behind the line of sending, not when the dog is entering the water or swimming. Create the impression in your dog that he did the right thing by getting in the water, but that there is hell to pay if he doesn't. Often a few swats with a stick and a verbal "Back, back, back!" or similar sequence with the e-collar will convince him that water is the place to be. This is remedial for the dog that has been forced on "Back" in the water.

Birds thrown from boats in open water, or in sparse cover, are often difficult. Boats seem to confuse dogs' memories. Most of this confusion can be alleviated by frequent practice on marks thrown from a boat. It doesn't need to be long or difficult, but it does require practice. Most dogs have trouble on their first mark thrown from a boat.

Running dogs from boats, or floating blinds, gives little trouble. The main thing is to teach them how to get in and out of the boat. Very little practice is required. We simply press down on the back of the dog's head or neck once he has placed his forefeet on the gunwale of the boat or the floor of a blind.

Rough, choppy water, or surf, call for special practice. Usually, good water dogs adapt quickly to new situations.

Much of North America, especially the coasts and the

Running water.

plains states, has a lot of shallow water. Shallow sloughs, potholes, tidal flats, and other such water are abundant. Most shallow water is lunging, or "running," water as we call it. Special practice is required in these places because, rather than being slowed down by having to swim, retrievers can move with speed. They tend to overrun birds that are partially submerged. Experienced dogs learn to check the area of the fall thoroughly in order to find such birds.

When handling dogs in running water, slipped whistles are likely. The racket caused by the dog's thrashing through the water drowns out the sound of the whistle.

It is a good idea, when practicing water marks, to establish a straight return as well as directness going out. This offers an opportunity to improve handling response as well as reinforcing going straight, which is especially important on water marks.

CAPPY

by John

ALTHOUGH WE WORK TO develop dogs' abilities, marking is mostly inherited, rather than a trained skill. The heights to which marking and memory can be developed in exceptional dogs is amazing.

One outstanding example was FC-AFC Capital City Jake (later a Dual Champion). In several trials, facing what appeared to be impossibly complicated marking tests, Cappy beat the field with precise marking beyond that which you would expect to see.

In one instance, the water quad at the end of an Open All-Age stake consisted of an arrangement of birds in an over-and-under configuration with two retired guns and a wipeout bird at close range. The handlers were doubtful that any of the remaining dogs could do the test "clean," that is, without handling on a mark. The professional trainer Billy Wunderlich pointed to Cappy and said, "They won't fool that sonofabitch." It didn't; Cappy completed the test perfectly and placed high in the trial.

It was not during competition that Cappy's talent for marking and memory got my attention. Although I did a good portion of Cappy's training after his purchase from the late Eloise Cherry, I didn't employ some of the tune-up procedures that my ex-wife, Jane, practiced when she was, for a time, on her own with Cappy. One evening, after sunset, at a National Amateur trial in Maine, Jane got Cappy out for a little marking drill.

She made Cappy sit and stay, then walked to the other side of a valley in the pasture where we were camped. When she reached the other side she walked to five different locations, throwing a dummy in the knee-high grass from each. The distances from Cappy's position ranged from 100 to 150 yards. Jane returned and sent Cappy for each dummy in turn. He marked them all unerringly.

I have never seen another dog demonstrate such complete mastery of marking, nor do I expect to see it again. Genius is rare.

CHAPTER 12

AGGRESSION

A S PROFESSIONAL TRAINERS, working with dogs of diverse pedigree and upbringing, we think we have some insight into the question of nature vs. nurture. We see some problems repeatedly connected with the same kind of training. The difficulty of resolving them depends to a large extent on how long they have been allowed to persist. These we put down to nurture. Inhibition of learning and/or retrieving as a consequence of too much early obedience is an example. We also see dogs with flaws that we may be able to improve somewhat, or compensate for by capitalizing on other abilities, but they rarely achieve high proficiency in the problem area. When these flaws appear regardless of the age we start working with the dog, and other dogs seem to excel in that area "right out of the box," we attribute the trait to inheritance. A vigorous, persistent hunt, or lack thereof, is an example of an inherent trait.

Predisposition to aggression is, in our opinion, largely a

matter of genes. This distinction is important because an aggressive dog requires lifelong management. We might reduce the incidence of aggression to zero with a combination of handling, training, and vigilance concerning situations that aggravate that behavior, but the need for our attentiveness will never go away.

A traditional, and permanent, solution to the problem of aggression is to get rid of the dog. An alternative is to hire a specialist consultant to help you set up a behavioral modification program. Armed with a thorough understanding of canine motivation, a good specialist can work wonders with a program tailor made for your dog. Their services are not cheap, and you must keep up the program for the life of your dog.

We have used both of the above options on a few dogs. Most often, however, we have followed a course of practical management, developed by trial and error. In our structured setting, this works with most retrievers.

Most aggression does not occur "out of the blue," but in a context that makes sense to the dog. When we consider the dog's ability to retaliate, we are amazed that dogs, particularly Labradors, do not bite more often. That they do not is a testament to the breeders who have rigorously selected for the desired temperament over many generations. Understanding the context of aggression, so that we can manage it, requires that we classify it correctly. Few dogs are indiscriminate biters; most aggressive animals fall into one or another category.

Some dogs are aggressive toward other dogs. The most familiar type is same-sex aggression between adults. Other dogs are aggressive toward puppies, and some react aggressively to the forwardness of another dog. Labs are sometimes attacked by other dogs that find them too forward.

Dogs can also be aggressive toward humans. We call it defensive aggression when a dog bites his trainer in response to training pressure. This occurs in all breeds but is especially characteristic of goldens. Resource guarding, where dogs growl, snarl, or bite in order to maintain possession of something of value, is another type. They may guard their food, toys, bones, or birds from people or other dogs. Some are inclined to guard an area, such as their yard, house, truck, or boat. Chesapeakes are known for this. Dogs may protect a person, and some have performed heroic feats saving a person from harm. Many times what is taken for protectiveness constitutes resource guarding where the person is the valued resource. In this case, they are likely to threaten or attack any dog or person that gets near the person they are guarding.

In cases of hostility toward other dogs, the assignment is always to keep them out of fights. Fights can be dangerous, both to the participants and to humans who intervene. Fighting dogs may bite anything at hand when in combat, including the hand that feeds them.

The most familiar form of aggression is that of one male toward another. Solid obedience is the best approach to controlling the problem. If "Here," "Heel," or "Sit" mean precisely that, with little chance of violation, most assaults can be prevented.

Temptations such as cats, squirrels, strange people, children, and ground scents (particularly bitch scent) can be used as enticements to violate the "Heel" or "Sit" command. When the rules are broken, a sufficiently stiff reinforcement with the e-collar, or other device, will serve to establish order. This must be repeated as many times as necessary until the dog remains in the heeling or sitting position no matter how great the temptation.

Expect that the requirement to remain at heel, or sitting, will carry over to your dog's truculent attitude toward others. In the event of failure to prevent your dog from fighting, you

Drilling on obedience around distractions.

are apt to find that much of the work you have done in this area will have to be redone. A general program of keeping your fight-inclined dog away from others except in working environments such as field trials or hunting is advised.

Building control, and understanding its limits, is essential. If your dog discovers that he can override your command to come or heel when called, he will be difficult to call away from a confrontation. Once he has been obedience trained, he can be gradually "proofed" around other dogs, starting by introducing inoffensive individuals at a distance during a lesson when his training responses are sharp. Call the dog and get control at the first sign of aggression. You need to learn to recognize the earliest sign, which is when the dog "orients," or focuses his attention on the prospective adversary. No matter how thorough the training, as aggression escalates, it becomes harder to regain control. To reinforce the idea of obedience in the presence of other dogs, it is necessary to interrupt aggression in its incipient stage and require obedience.

Once the behavior of challenging or fighting with other dogs in the working setting has become established, direct pressure, especially that administered with the e-collar, yields poor results. More often the commotion and agitation created by corrective measures escalate the combat. Mature dogs that have developed the fighting pattern must be removed from temptation while obedience is reinforced. Shielding the fighter from challenges by others is a good idea.

We have known a few male retrievers that have never been

trustworthy around other dogs. The mere sight of another male was enough to put them beyond the reach of command. In some cases, only certain males provoked an aggressive response; dogs have definite dislikes. Fighters tend to carry their tails high and demonstrate deliberate, self-directed behavior at all times. When allowed, they sniff the ground in a deliberate way. When we see this combination of traits, we keep them away from other males.

Some fight only if attacked, but then are devastating. The assailant seems to recognize the potential for battle in this type and can't resist the challenge.

You can't fault a dog for defending himself, but when the result is severe injury or possibly death to the attacking dog, measures should be taken to warn owners of the liabilities of their behavior. John once had a Chesapeake, Pilot, who didn't start fights, but once involved, would lock onto his opponent's head with a bulldog-like grip, and not let go until his jaws were pried open with a tool, like a screwdriver. The best bet with this type is to keep him away from other dogs and warn their owners of the problem.

Hostility among bitches is somewhat rarer than in males. Females are typically more laid back. Those who do fight, however, are frequently effective fighters, and may confront males as well as other females. They must be fully obedient, just like males. Fighters of either sex must never be left unsupervised with potential opponents.

Some bitches, and some dogs, will attack small puppies

other than their own. In these cases the attack is likely to cause the death of the puppy. The undesired action usually takes place when a puppy sidles up to the strange adult for attention, having no idea what is coming.

Aggression toward people may occur in the absence of aggression toward other dogs, or one individual may display both. Defensive aggression, as we said, is when the dog threatens or bites the handler in response to, or fear of, something the dog doesn't like. During training this is usually correction or pressure. Often the dog is stable in other respects, but reacts by protecting itself from the treatment it dislikes. It may bite in response to an ear or toe pinch, or to collar or stick pressure. We do not beat or otherwise punish dogs after the fact, but expect that biting could occur under those circumstances. Dogs may also bite when their trainer reaches for their collar or puts a collar on, or reaches into its kennel to get the dog. We remove potential biters from their run on a slip lead (the noose may be put around the dog's head without getting too close), then put a collar on.

We want dogs to think about their training, not how to avoid it. If they threaten to bite, we work out a less confrontational program to accomplish our goal. Usually some pressure will be needed, but the amount of pressure, rate of advancement, and length of sessions may need to be adjusted. We watch the dog closely for indications that it understands that it can "turn off" pressure. We proceed with caution, going slow rather than rushing.

While our opinion is that a tendency to defend itself is or is not inborn, dogs are subject to conditioning either to be apprehensive and bite readily, or to respond as trained and bite only as a last resort. Dogs trained in a confrontational manner, if they are defensive biters, will sometimes snap or bite at the first sign of pressure. Dogs who are trained to turn off pressure by the correct response are less hair-triggered.

Some dogs are more apprehensive. Apprehensiveness may not be obvious. We had a Lab in training who seemed generally recalcitrant and uncooperative. When he started snapping at us for little provocation, we videotaped him and mailed the tape to an aggression specialist. Only after she pointed out his mannerisms showing fear and apprehension did we recognize them. Like other fearful dogs we have worked with, this dog learned little and we sent him home as a washout.

Dogs that are fearful in a kennel setting may do better at home. If they are generally fearful, a force program may increase their fear. For owners who choose to keep dogs of this type, training by positive reinforcement may be a better and safer alternative. It is important, not only to avoid being bitten, but to minimize the chance of your dog's biting someone else. Positive reinforcement training is less likely to aggravate apprehension. Hunting dogs must travel to do their job, so adaptability to strange surroundings is essential. Putting your dog in a situation where it is apprehensive with strangers approaching and expecting it to be friendly, is dangerous.

Fear and apprehensiveness in unfamiliar surroundings or

around strangers can result from inadequate socialization as a puppy. The chapter on puppies describes remedial socialization for adult dogs.

Possessiveness over food or toys is common among Chesapeakes and occurs in others as well. This is dangerous in the home, especially if children get too close to the dog's food or toy. We have heard of several scary incidents. Many Chesapeake owners manage the problem by isolating their dogs while feeding, and keeping toys in the crate.

Feeding time may be an occasion for aggression.

We do have experience training dogs with a history of possessive aggression. Like all of our trainees, these dogs are kept in the controlled environment of our kennel. They are fed in the kennel, at the same time every day, and have a couple of training sessions each day. Some of these dogs, by their owners' account, will threaten anyone who gets within a few feet of their dish while they are eating. Eventually, all of our trainees will accept our picking up their feed pan when they are half-finished. Typically, we try this when they have been here a month, by which time we have had our hands on their mouths, teaching them to hold and release a dummy. The controlled environment, structured schedule, and consistent training make them relax. We do not subscribe to "dominating" dogs. We begin training gently, and remain focused on teaching, not domination.

Some dogs will fence-fight over their supper. We do not allow this, so we move dogs around in the kennel until the problem stops. Some dogs have specific dislikes, and will behave when given different neighbors, while others need to be isolated.

Some trained retrievers aggressively prevent interference while working. We have seen this in some Chesapeake bitches with considerable drive and motivation. One was on a blind retrieve when a local dog got in her path, trying to play. *Snap snap snap snap snap* she drove him away and continued on the line she was taking. Another, while hunting with her owner, bit a hunting partner who tried to take a bird from her. She reacted to the violation of established practice.

Chesapeakes, especially, may drive another dog away from a bird they have found. Again, our chief recommendation is prevention. You don't want a dog fight. Retrievers deserve the opportunity to make retrieves without interference. Unless the other dog is trained to honor, work your retriever alone.

As we mentioned above, a dog may also possessively guard a person. This may be mistaken for protectiveness, but is a nuisance as the dog threatens or attacks any other dog that gets close. As with other forms of aggression, thorough obedience training helps. Your dog cannot lunge at another dog while sitting at heel. Avoid situations where uncontrolled dogs are likely to run up to you. This applies any time you are working a dog—when you require the dog to pay attention to you, it is your responsibility to protect him from hazards in the environment.

Retrievers of all breeds may be protective of home and family. Sometimes it is not easy to tell if this is a matter of resource guarding, of fear, or threat to a family member. A Chesapeake of our breeding was once riding in the back seat of a vehicle when carjackers struck. She remained still as three men approached and tried to open the doors. When one man put his arm through the open passenger-side window to unlock the door, the dog's owner gasped in fear, and the dog instantly rounded the front passenger seat and sank her teeth into the offender's arm. She did quite a bit of damage, broke up the carjacking, and was much admired by the police when they arrived. We do not know precisely why she bit the carjacker;

was she frightened, possessive, or protecting her owner? The result was good, but might have been disastrous if the carjackers had had guns, or if a friend getting into the car had provoked an attack. You cannot depend on a dog to make all of the right calls on his own. He's bound to make costly mistakes along the line. We recommend that protective tendencies not be allowed to develop unchecked.

Biting dogs are a liability. Since aggressive behavior is largely an inherited trait, we can help to prevent it by selecting our puppies from breedings of good temperament. If the problem exists, face it squarely and as early in your puppy's life as possible, or you may find yourself faced with the option of putting down an otherwise excellent prospect.

CAPPY'S AGGRESSION

by John

THERE ARE, AS THEY SAY, two sides to every coin. In the case of dogs, one side might be a plus, and the other a debilitating fault. Such was the case with the Chesapeake, Cappy, about whom I have written elsewhere in this book.

A few dogs, particularly those who are strong-willed characters, whose notion that they are right in all situations is unshakeable, take a proprietary attitude toward everything in their surrounding. This may include their home, yard, a choice sleeping spot, a vehicle, birds, holding blind, the path to the line at a field trial and, yes, even their handler.

Cappy fell into this category with some to spare. The birds were his. This included encroachment from other dogs, or men. They were guarded as personal property. Even Cappy's owner suffered a minor bite when she went out in the dark one night to reprimand Cappy for hassling some ducks in a crate. Probably in the dark and in his preoccupation with the birds, he didn't recognize the human interloper. On another occasion, Cappy attacked a crate of ducks on his way off the line in an Open stake he had clearly won. The result was his getting dropped from the trial for bad manners, lack of control, or something. It didn't seem to me to be a definable offense; some judges would have let it go.

The worst aspect of Cappy's aggressive behavior was not with birds but in his fighting proclivities. On three occasions that I can recall, he attacked a dog during a field trial. Two of them occurred while under judgment, which eliminated him from future A.K.C. trials.

The circumstances of these attacks involved his being handled by Jane in trials. It always appeared to me that his motives were protective, and the more vigorously she tried to prevent the behavior, the more intense the aggression became.

Fighting is one of the most difficult things to train a dog not to do. Like many traits, it is inherited. Chesapeakes and goldens show a markedly higher tendency to fight than do Labs. Dog fights are hazardous not only to the participants, but also to people who may be in close proximity to the conflict. Fighting should not be condoned, nor tolerated.

Cappy had spectacular talent—and an All-Age career that lasted just over a year because of his aggression.

CHAPTER 13

SPECIAL PUPPY CONCERNS

MANY PROBLEMS, some of them difficult to treat, become apparent in puppies between six weeks and six months of age. Some symptoms may be accidental, or are due to their stage of development and are likely to disappear with age. Physical and mental immaturity account for most of the behavior you see. There are many things you can do to help your youngster to adjust to life and prepare him for the excellence you hope to achieve.

Some puppy activities are the beginnings of bad habits, and should be minimized. Other behavior may indicate flaws or unusual personality types, such as shy or independent dispositions, which may be moderated by proper handling. We will discuss a variety of puppy behavior, give suggestions as to what you can do to improve the situation in the short run, and recommend how to achieve the best outcome in the long run. Thus armed, we hope you will be able to relax and enjoy your puppy.

The retrieving instinct shows up early—but puppies still need training to become good retrievers.

Running away with the retrieving dummy or bird

As long as your puppy eagerly goes after the retrieving object, coming back is not something to worry about. Almost all puppies, after having learned to retrieve, will at some point stop bringing the dummy back. They may run off to play keep-away, or parade in circles, buzzing past you every so often to make sure you are paying attention. They may act possessive, even growling as they whisk their prize out of your reach. We consider this a good sign; recently we raised an otherwise nice puppy who consistently retrieved to hand up to the age of five months. We worried about him. When he started doing longer marks in the field, the "keep-away" response finally kicked in and we were glad to see it. Playfulness after getting the dummy seems to be a spillover of

Running off is normal—especially when retrieving birds.

a puppy's enthusiasm for pursuing and finding the object, and is indicative of good drive.

There are short-term and long-term repercussions of letting your puppy's games of keep-away go unchecked. The long-term problem is to avoid developing a habit so strong that severe training will be needed to overcome it. There is a cost to the working relationship when entrenched problems are attacked head-on using force. This means that unless you can find a way to get your puppy back following a retrieve, you will have to suspend retrieving until you can formally train him to come back. With some puppies, a little gentle work on coming when called is sufficient. For most it is not. They may come at all other times, but not when they have a dummy. Or they may do a perfect retrieve the first time, and on the next retrieve, run out to the dummy, seem to realize that picking it up means they must bring it to you, and leave it on the ground. Some will get the dummy, but spit it out the moment they are called.

If your puppy always comes when called, but without the dummy, you will probably have to force fetch before doing more retrieving. We recommend waiting until the adult teeth are fully in before beginning work on "hold" and "fetch." This is the reason we specify *gentle* work on coming-when-called. If your puppy is one that will come at other times but runs off during retrieves, you will be able to continue retrieving practice using check cords and a variety of creative measures.

Since getting puppies back on retrieves is a standard part of training, we described strategies in detail in our book on basic training, *The 10-Minute Retriever.* We cover them more briefly here. Check cords are straightforward. We like braided polypropylene cord because it is relatively resistant to tangling, and have used lengths of 100 feet and more. With most puppies, a cord long enough to step on as the puppy zooms by is all that is needed; a few determined escapees may be confined to retrieves within the length of the longest cord you can manage.

Throws straight into water or cover will get many puppies to return, as they usually want to take the shortest route out of the hazard, and that is back by you. A short check cord you can step on goes well with this strategy.

Puppies also tend to head from the unknown back to the familiar. In an unfamiliar field, they frequently head back to the car or truck (and under it—again that check cord is use-ful). If you throw in a direction that positions you in the puppy's return path, you have a good chance to catch him. In your yard, you can try standing by an open door to the house, or to your puppy's outdoor pen or kennel if you have one.

Some puppies will need these measures up until the time they are formally trained. Some will give in to the control, and re-establish the habit of returning to you. Quite a few of the good ones will put added effort into avoiding you. They may learn the exact length of their check cord and stay a few inches beyond your reach, or dash off to the side in the shallow water to prevent your catching them as they come ashore. You are not going to hurt their prospects by taking a break from retrieving until after they are force-fetched, if retrieving prac-tice becomes too much hassle. Obviously their enthusiasm is well-established, and that is the main point in retrieving work with puppies.

Puppies who begin running off at a very early age (or never retrieve to you), and those who head straight in the other direction without trying to tease you into a game of keep-away are unusually independent individuals. We describe our method for building responsiveness in an independent puppy in the story about Stormy following this chapter.

Roughness with birds/Possessiveness with birds
It is normal for puppies with their milk teeth to bite down hard on birds. It is also normal for puppies to be reluctant to

give birds up. Commonly, enthusiasm for birds "switches on" suddenly, and the associated excitement seems to overwhelm the puppy. Puppies may run off with their birds, tear feathers out, repeatedly toss the bird in the air, or return with the bird but growl or simply lock their jaws so that they seem impossible to pry apart. All of this is good—it means the puppy is birdy. Avoid punishing puppies for mishandling birds. As long as the puppy does not have enough opportunities to establish a habit of roughing up birds, bird handling will be much better when bird work resumes after force fetching.

Focus should be on sufficient exposure to birds without excessive opportunities to practice mishandling them. We recommend throwing birds for puppies once every week or two. Use only well-feathered pigeons or ducks that are in good condition. A check cord can be used if needed to recall your puppy. Most puppies will release a bird when they are picked up; if not, their mouths are easier to pry open when you are holding them.

If your puppy is so wild about birds that you cannot get him to return, stop using birds and work exclusively with dummies. His desire for birds has been established, and more mishandling of them could become habitual.

Disobedience

It is common for little puppies to respond very quickly to gentle, informal obedience training. With only a little praise and petting, and a few repetitions, many are easily taught to sit, stay, and come when called. Not only do they learn quickly, they respond reliably in a variety of settings. Later, often suddenly, obedience may fail. The puppy acts distracted and ignores commands, especially from a distance. This, too, is normal. Don't take it personally. It does not mean your puppy does not love you, is defying you, is becoming untrainable, or has aspirations to "dominance."

At varying ages, puppies become less dependent upon their human and more involved with other aspects of their environment. Their eyes and noses are improving, they are getting stronger and more coordinated, and they need to exercise these capabilities. This is good. Dogs that are overly dependent on their owners might make good pets, but lack initiative.

The informal training that worked with younger puppies loses effectiveness with the emerging explorer. It doesn't pay to punish puppies when they ignore commands. It might help to revisit obedience training, incorporating corrections, and gradually incorporating distractions to improve reliability. We prefer another approach, however. Some owners seem to fear their puppies will become headstrong if not taught early, but obedience is easy to establish at five or six months in a well-socialized puppy. The best results in later training are obtained by encouraging your puppy to explore and follow his impulses—with you nearby to gently steer him away from bad habits.

Go out with your puppy as often as you can. Take him somewhere new and safe, where he can explore off lead. This makes you the key to his greatest satisfactions. Learn to recognize times when he is not preoccupied with the new surroundings, call him, pat and praise him, then release him to play again. This fosters a solid foundation for a positive training attitude.

You will fail to hold your puppy's attention if other dogs are present. Free play with dogs impairs a puppy's trainability. Owners mistakenly think such interaction is good for their puppy. A few contacts with adult dogs known to be gentle with puppies may help teach good manners around dogs, but playing must not be allowed to become a high priority.

The pitfalls of puppy raising are suppressing initiative with too much control or punishment, failing to socialize, and formation of bad habits. Habits are formed through repetition. There is no need to punish puppies on the first offense. Prevent recurrences and ensure that the behavior is not rewarded. If the puppy winds between your legs, stand with your feet together. If he jumps up on family members, make sure nobody praises him for it. There are more detailed suggestions in Chapter 15, on Manners.

Puppy biting

Retriever puppies like to bite. We have tried a number of ways to discourage puppy biting, including waiting for it to go away on its own (painful). The method we now use beats everything else we have tried. We recommend it highly. We call it "Just say Ow!" It boils down to teaching a puppy to be gentle by imitating another puppy's response to pain.

Puppies appear to have a built-in mechanism for moderating their bite. Eight-week-old retriever puppies that are with

This puppy, which has not yet been taken from its litter, bites very gently.

their littermates are, with few exceptions, gentle. Take them from the litter, however, and they soon bite harder. And harder. Waiting for the biting to go away on its own works, but puppies bite hard enough to draw blood. Back when we punished puppies for biting, by bopping them on the nose or shaking them by the scruff, their response was often to react by biting quicker and harder. Now we give a high-pitched "Ow!" imitating the yipe a bitten littermate might give, and withhold attention (take our hands away) for a few seconds. The response is usually a gentler bite. Puppies will gauge how hard a bite is acceptable. We can repeat our "Ow!" response, and further decrease biting pressure. We have "tuned" puppies' biting down to almost nothing with a small number of repetitions. One or a few instances have worked with Lab and Chesapeake puppies we've raised.

We think that several popular notions that supposedly implement dog nature in training are useless and misleading. This is particularly the case with trainer attempts to imitate an "alpha wolf." On the other hand, when we can be successful by taking advantage of a dog's natural "programming," as we do to decrease painful biting, we can be more effective trainers. The distinction is between assumptions misapplied, and techniques developed through practical experience.

The "just say 'ow!'" approach is easy, harmonious, and omits punishment, setting the stage for a better training relationship.

Leash pulling

We discuss correcting leash pulling in our chapter on Manners. Puppies can usually be prevented from developing the habit, however. If you are careful to make sure that your puppy is never hauled around or allowed to pull steadily against the leash, he is likely not to learn to pull. Keep any tightening of the leash as brief as possible. We achieve this by holding the hand loop of a six-foot lead and letting the puppy do the rest. Typically they hit the end of the lead a few times, bounce back, and learn to avoid it. We may have to give the puppy a quick tug back into the "slack zone" to prevent his continuing a steady pull. You might find this easier with a longer lead. Remember to hold it by its end, and resist the temptation to pull on your puppy.

Retractable leads encourage pulling, and we don't recommend them.

Thanks to good early socialization, this puppy relaxes when held.

Timidity

Fearful or shy-acting puppies require prompt intervention. Retrievers must be adaptable; they can learn to go anywhere and do their job. If your retriever doesn't adapt to strange places and people, training in groups is ruled out and hunting opportunities will be limited. Fearful or apprehensive dogs are much more likely to bite. This is particularly dangerous in a Labrador or golden, two breeds that strangers take for granted as friends.

Whether a dog is reticent by nature or just poorly socialized, the treatment is the same: thoroughly socialize the puppy. In young puppies, six to eight weeks old, we start by teaching them to accept human handling. First we stroke the head and back. We hold them gently, waiting for them to relax, then set them down.

We do not recommend rough handling with puppies, especially timid ones—no pinning the puppy on its back, shaking by the scruff, or shouting. The goal is to build the puppy's trust and confidence in humans, and his comfort in different surroundings. Gradually increase exposure to humans and as wide a variety of experiences as you can. Create favorable associations with threatening stimuli, such as strangers.

Typical retriever puppies go through a phase during which they are fearless of new experiences. Sights, sounds, smells, and categories of people, introduced during this time, will be taken in stride later in life. We advise people to handle and hold their puppy a lot, take it to a variety of places, and have it meet a variety of people (pre-screened for their ability to treat puppies properly). With those that are already showing signs of fearfulness, a more structured program is needed. This is particularly true after four to six months of age.

Food can be used to create favorable associations with previously threatening stimuli. Most retrievers are enthusiastic about food. This is a good time to capitalize on that. When you have a problem, food may be your most potent weapon. Food treats don't have to be large. One food treat that is compatible with most diets is ½" cubes of boiled chicken. Other things retrievers like are hotdog pieces, liver, and high-calorie food supplements, which are sold in tubes at pet-supply houses.

Make a target list of things you want your puppy to accept. Include strangers, the car, the vet's office, and other such places. These might include your neighborhood side-walks, areas you will train, your boat, and the local boarding kennel. With each, you want to begin at a low level of exposure so that your puppy is not overwhelmed by fear, and gradually increase.

To work on fear of strangers, begin by finding a new helper. Put your puppy wherever he is most comfortable in the house. Position yourself by the puppy, and have your helper come in and sit on the opposite side of the room for about a minute, then leave. Feed your puppy treats while the stranger is present. Stop when they leave. After several minutes, have your helper return briefly, and feed your puppy treats as before. If your puppy reacts by looking for treats when the stranger comes in, have them stay longer.

Once you establish a starting point, you can increase the exposure by having the person stay longer. Move toward your helper so your puppy must come with you to get the treats. Eventually you can sit next to the "stranger," allowing them to give the treats. Then try to get your puppy to let the stranger touch him. When your puppy eagerly greets your helper and accepts being handled by them, introduce another new person.

Use a similar approach to conditioning your puppy to being near the car, being in the car, being in the car with the engine running, and going for a quick ride around the block. Once your puppy willingly enters the car, you can take him to new places. Many public places are deserted in the early morning, and you can familiarize your dog with them without exposing him to crowds. As your puppy becomes comfortable, you can return during busier times.

We have described a procedure for a very fearful puppy. Most shy retrievers are not at this level. With most, you can progress more quickly to all forms of exposure. We still recommend repeating with a variety of people in different places. Dogs are frequently frightened by people in hats, people in uniform, and people of different race than their owners. You may want to include these in your program.

Puppy quits retrieving

By "quitting," we mean stopping picking up the dummy or bird. Puppies often stop coming back, but if they pick up the object, they aren't quitting, and the solutions are different. There are two prevalent causes of quitting: too much emphasis on obedience, or teething. Occasionally, some other health problem is the cause.

Problems with teething are easy to spot. A puppy that has been gung-ho up to the age of four or four and a half months will suddenly drop the dummy, then run out but not pick it up, then quit retrieving altogether. You can usually see tender areas on his gums, loose teeth, and new teeth coming in. You may be able to keep him retrieving using small birds or soft toys. We usually take a retrieving break until the gums heal. Some puppies retrieve right through the teething period, sometimes bringing back bumpers covered with blood. Most don't.

The most common cause of puppies quitting retrieving is

too much obedience training. Getting puppies started retrieving again, when there has been a lot of punishment or premature steadying, is problematic. Too much time spent on obedience can put a stop to retrieving even when no punishment or shouting is involved. Expecting near-perfect reliability and control from a young puppy is a mistake. There is no advantage to it—obedience can be delayed until six months or so. There is a big disadvantage, though, in the missed chance to build a puppy's confidence and initiative.

When a puppy quits retrieving, is not teething, and appears otherwise healthy, we advise the owner to stop obedience and all attempts to retrieve for two weeks. The puppy should not be shouted at or punished for transgressions in the home, either. Then try to get the puppy retrieving in a situation as far removed from past lessons as is practical. A new retrieving object and location, and if possible, a different handler, all improve the chance of success. Sponges, stuffed toys, and paint rollers make good retrieving objects. Highly visible colors are best.

If a new person is to handle the puppy, the original trainer should not be present. The puppy should be allowed out to explore, wearing a buckle collar instead of a training collar. After a few minutes, get his attention and introduce the new retrieving object. If he mouths the toy, say, "Good, good" then toss it a few feet, making sure the toy stays within the puppy's view. If he shows no interest, gently tease the puppy with the object until he grabs for it. Sometimes restraining puppies gently by the collar helps them focus on the toy. A little tug of war may help develop his interest. After throwing the object, the handler turns his back. This is important if the original trainer is doing the reintroduction. Direct attention is inhibiting, especially on the pickup. If the puppy appears with the object, the handler should praise and make a fuss over him, repeat twice, and call it a day. Don't worry about delivery, and don't give a command to retrieve. Try to re-teach the puppy that retrieving is a fun. Burdening him with associated requirements is a mistake.

If the puppy does not pick up the object, go to it, pick it up and play with it. When he comes to investigate, try once again to get him interested.

The next session, the handler should try to restrain the dog by the collar for about a second after the throw, letting him go

Restraining a puppy as she watches the throw helps build enthusiasm.

before the object hits the ground. Limit the session to three throws, and don't use commands or insist on delivery to hand. Continue with daily sessions until the puppy is retrieving eagerly as far as you can throw. At this point, the original trainer can try to get him to retrieve, in the new location. Restrain the puppy until the object almost reaches the ground. Continue to use restraint, and avoid imposing requirements on delivery, until he is force fetched. The command to retrieve can now be given as the puppy is released.

We have reactivated many dogs' retrieving with this approach, and have reports from many owners who used it successfully. If the puppy was an eager retriever before, he will be again. Puppies may misunderstand their training and think they should not retrieve. The reason punishment is so apt to cause problems is that puppies don't understand it nearly so well as we think. We may inadvertently cause fear and inhibition.

Sloppy hold

Force fetching improves a sloppy hold, but we don't want it to be more of an ordeal than necessary. Insofar as possible, we try to establish a good hold in puppy retrieves.

We prefer to tweak the circumstances to favor developing good habits, without imposing rigid requirements. The best way to achieve a good carry varies with the individual. We start puppies that have a firm grip early with plastic dummies. Puppies soon learn that they can carry the dummy easily by holding it in the middle. By the time they are old enough to force fetch, a proper hold has become habitual. We see few problems with cigar holds or dummies dangling from their mouths.

Some dogs lack a firm grip. As puppies, they can't carry a plastic dummy without repeatedly dropping it. The effort to hold it is too great. Within some distance from the handler, they drop it and come in without it. With such dogs, a lighter object with a more appealing texture may work. A rolled-up sock, a paint roller, or a plush toy work well for little puppies. Older ones can retrieve a puppy-sized canvas dummy. Don't use toys that squeak, as they encourage repeated biting down.

Emerging from the water while carrying a dummy presents a challenge. A dog suddenly has to work harder to hold the dummy, once the water no longer supports it, and he will shake. Prior to force-fetching, meet your puppy at the water's edge and take the dummy before he drops it.

In hot weather, dogs pant to cool themselves. Puppies are particularly bothered by heat. If your puppy delivers well in the cool of the morning but not in the hot afternoon, work when it is cool. It doesn't take much to overheat a retriever, even on a cool day. This is one of the reasons for short training sessions. Experience and force fetching will clear the way for greater discipline.

Difficulty learning new things; inhibitions

Some dogs are not too bright. Males don't learn as readily after being castrated (spaying females does not appear to have a similar effect). Most of the time, however, failure to progress is a training problem. There are two common causes: excessive punishment, and failure to move ahead at the right time.

Retriever trainers employ force using sticks, e-collars, ear and toe pinches, etc. These are most effective and cause fewest side effects when applied as "pressure," that is, to initiate rather than alter behavior. Using them as punishment for unwanted behavior often has undesirable effects. Dogs may refuse to get in the water if they have been punished there; they may develop inhibition about trying new things; they may become fearful of taking one particular cast or another action that they associated with the punishment. In a regimen of "pressure to go" it is both safer and more effective to discourage wrong behavior using attrition. Attrition means stopping the dog without punishment, calling him back to some prior point in the sequence, and requiring him to try again.

When young puppies are subjected to an excess of punishment (how much is too much varies with the individual), they can become reluctant to try new things. We can usually remedy this, but it adds to the time needed to achieve the owner's goals. Gentle early preparation facilitates smooth progress.

Some dogs get stuck at a particular phase of training because of excess repetition. Some dogs have gone for months with nothing but hand throws. It is hard to get them retrieving from a distant thrower. Pattern work is often overdone. Novice trainers sometimes seek perfection at every level. More experienced trainers judge when dogs understand well enough to move on, even if they still make occasional mistakes. Dogs' willingness to try new things is maintained by consistent advancement. Sometimes, because of lack of access to grounds, owners overwork drills. Some dogs stagnate so badly that progress is halted.

Lack of interest in birds

Very young retrievers are usually birdy. When they are not exposed to birds early, it can take more effort to wake up bird interest. The important thing is to get the puppy to pick up the bird. It doesn't take much bird exposure for the puppy to become enthusiastic about them. If teasing the puppy with a bird then tossing it does not cause him to pick it up, try standing with the bird dangling in your hand and the puppy at large. Sometimes puppies will sniff and mouth the bird, and then start tugging to get it away. Let him have it! If he carries it around, try throwing it again.

If your puppy does not pick the bird up in the first session, try again with a fresh bird another day. Don't get discouraged if two or three sessions go by without success. We have had dogs go for over a week showing no interest, then one day they pick up the bird and everything changes.

Housebreaking failures

We advocate the "crate training" approach to housebreaking puppies. It makes use of the puppy's natural behavior to teach him when and where to relieve himself. If you are not using the crate method, and you are having problems, our best advice is to get a crate and start using it.

We describe the method in detail in *The 10-Minute Retriever*. In brief, since puppies are inhibited about soiling the small space where they are confined, confinement induces your puppy to "hold it" for a period of time, making it probable that he will relieve himself when you take him straight from the crate to your designated spot. Then you can anticipate that he will be clean for a while, give him some house time, and put him back in the crate before he needs to go again. Regular meals and water are necessary.

Go out with your puppy, no matter what the weather. This will help you avoid a dirty crate.

Puppy in a crate.

Usually, puppies can make it through the night without going out by the time they are nine or ten weeks old. If yours cannot, you can try adjusting his feeding schedule, or his food. Some dog foods produce greater stool volume, and more bowel movements per day, than others. Some lead to softer stools, and hence less control. We have had good results feeding a high quality puppy food and allowing several hours between the evening feeding and the puppy's final outing of the day.

Some puppies will urinate in their crates without notification. Sometimes removing bedding will solve this problem. Dogs are inclined to urinate on an absorbent surface. Some will urinate on a dog bed if it is in their crate. If it is removed, they control themselves and bark to get out.

STORMY

by Amy

S TORMY IS A CHESAPEAKE of our own breeding. She first showed her independence very early, at three or four weeks of age. Retrievers of an independent nature are difficult to train, as they don't seem to care whether the trainer likes their behavior or not. If a dog is not cooperating the results will be poor. Stormy didn't seem to develop a desire to cuddle or be held. She never "retrieved" as a puppy. She learned at just over five weeks to run out and pick up an object, but had no inclination to return with it. As she got bigger and stronger, she would pick up the dummy or bird I threw and run to the woods with it. On off-lead walks, she ranged far out, without occasionally "checking in" the way others will. I was concerned she might grow up to be a difficult adult.

I worked especially hard to get Stormy to associate me with everything good in her life. It was discouraging, as she didn't respond much at first. I took her for twice daily off-lead walks. She didn't pay me the attention other puppies do, although she did keep track of where I was, and returned when I headed home. I was able to get her to come, some of the time, for tasty treats like boiled liver. I threw dummies or birds for Stormy every day. After throwing one, I would wait until she finished playing with it and came back, then throw the next one. At the end of the session I picked up the dummies she had left out; sometimes I would put Stormy away and get another retriever to hunt them up. Stormy was not interested in keep-away games; she merely took her dummies farther away if I went after her.

When Stormy was small, I held her every day. As she got bigger, I petted and brushed her. I taught her to sit and come for liver treats. I tried to make sure that I was part of her fun. When it came time for formal obedience and force fetching, Stormy did OK. She did require two months to force fetch, longer than most puppies we raise ourselves. Since beginning field work, she has behaved normally. She solicits attention like any other Chesapeake, responds well to training, and acts affectionate.

Stormy was not much fun to raise, because she didn't reward the work I put into her with affection or cute behavior. Still, we think it is a good idea, if a puppy shows an extreme personality type, to make an effort to moderate it.

CHAPTER 14

FORCE FETCHING PROBLEMS

FORCE FETCHING RETRIEVERS is difficult, especially when you lack experience. When a dog does not respond, do you need to apply more pressure, less pressure, ease up on requirements, shorten the session, or perhaps bear down and keep trying until he gets it? Even experienced trainers can find it hard to read a dog that is doing nothing.

To force fetch more efficiently, with less distress to both dog and trainer, consider what you are trying to accomplish. You want the dog to "fetch" from the ground on command, reliably, carry dummies and birds without dropping or mishandling them, and deliver properly. Finally, you are teaching a constructive response to "pressure" for use in future training. The majority of force-fetching struggles arise from the trainer's failure to recognize that dogs do not automatically understand pressure. You must teach the dog that he can make the pressure stop by finding the right response. While some dogs can be force fetched in a few days, others must be taken slowly, to bol-

Force fetching ensures reliable deliveries.

ster the notion that they can, through their responses, control what happens to them.

Many of us have heard that noncompliance means dogs are resisting and require convincing that the trainer's will is law. We no longer wholly agree with this interpretation. If force is involved, we think refusals most often mean that the training foundation is inadequate. Either the action called for is over his head, or he does not understand that he can "turn off the pressure" by his response, or both. Obvious as the required action is to us, we have failed to get the message across.

A question we have not yet answered is whether resistance is essential to force-fetching success. Force fetching is something of a black box—the focus is on bringing retrieving under the trainer's control, but along the way other things happen. Most notably, obedience improves sharply. We don't know exactly what causes this. We have had some retrievers, particularly bitches, come through force fetching smoothly, with little resistance. But when we attempted field work, we found that the force-fetching didn't "take." The retrievers in question failed to deliver properly, dropped dummies, refused to pick them up, and did not demonstrate the anticipated gain in overall compliance. When we returned to force fetching, we encountered resistance, worked through it, then achieved the desired results. Does this indicate that we must provoke and overcome resistance in order to get a dog thoroughly force-fetched?

We don't operate on the notion that dogs defy us or want to take control. We do find that some "test" us, trying out options other than compliance. When dogs test us during force-fetching, where we have control over the dog, the effect carries over into field work. Some resistance may be conducive to thorough force-fetching. Persistent refusals, however, usually call for simplification of the process.

Having described the assumptions with which we approach force fetching, we now turn to specific problems.

Extraneous Responses

Some dogs try to escape pressure from the ear pinch or toe hitch by struggling to get away, lying down, or biting. While we are sympathetic to dogs who fail to grasp the reason for the discomfort, we must teach them that they can succeed only by taking the dummy in their mouths. As long as dogs think they can stop pressure by other means, they will not develop the habit we are trying to instill.

If you are force fetching on the ground and your retriever is solid on the "Sit" command, repeating "Sit" with a correction will often do the trick. Some otherwise obedient retrievers, however, are so upset by the ear pinch that prior training seems to escape them. Physical restraint is effective for removing options, and lessens attempts to escape pressure by struggling. We train without restraint when possible, and we reward correct responses with a break and some heeling. If it doesn't work, we use restraint.

There are a variety of ways to restrain dogs. Some truss them to a bench or table. Usually they are restrained by the neck, sometimes with a strap around the belly as well. We use solid tables, but other trainers say that a less stable bench reduces resistance. Restraints may be attached to a plywood board behind the table, or to a cable or shelf above the dog.

Working on a table is easier on the trainer's back, but you can also restrain dogs on the ground. You can stretch a cable between two trees and construct a fixed point to attach his collar with a bolt snap. An oversized collar strap, for his belly, may be added. Thus restrained, most dogs will soon focus on the desired response—taking the dummy.

Fighting the pressure occurs mostly early during force fetching. Sometimes it starts when we try to make them pick up dummies from the ground. Instead of struggling with these dogs, we use a restraint that allows them to pick up

Restraint limits the dog's options, so he is more likely to fetch.

dummies from the ground, but little else. It consists of two check cords attached to separate buckle collars. One check cord is attached to a tree, and we hold, or stand on, the other. Confined by cords stretching in opposite directions, a retriever can lower his head to the ground, but can do little else to escape pressure. We have been successful, by keeping the cords taught, in preventing dogs from reaching us to bite. We acknowledge, however, that there are probably dogs that are more inclined to bite than those we have trained, and urge caution in training any dog that displays aggression. We do not respond directly to attempts to bite. We use restraints and heavy gloves for protection, adjust pressure, and reduce difficulty to promote the desired response—fetching—over biting.

Occasionally dogs resist vigorously when force-fetching is almost complete. We have found that if we reduce our demands and give them opportunities to succeed, they will usually cooperate. Their struggles seem to say, "I get it! Let me show you."

Dogs intolerant of restraint

We sometimes put dogs on the table from the start. Most adjust quickly, or struggle a little and give up, but a few seem to panic. Sometimes a vigorous fight will cause them to escape the belly strap. Frightened dogs have difficulty learning, and may be better off on the ground. Methods that work on most dogs won't necessarily work on all. If yours doesn't respond "by the book," don't give up. Retriever personalities vary widely. Adapting to individual requirements pays off.

Thus far we have not had to go from the ground to the table and back to the ground again. We have, however, had a small number of dogs we thought might have trouble with both approaches. With these we spent several days introducing the table setup, starting with only a loose collar restraint. We created favorable associations, using treats and pats, and kept initial exposure to the table brief. The belly strap was introduced with more petting and treats. In a few days these dogs were jumping onto the table and accepting restraint. We don't know what the results would have been if we'd trained these dogs differently, but all showed fearfulness similar to the ones that panicked.

Dog objects to pressure and/or the initial fetch response is hard to establish

Most dogs get the basic idea of fetching in response to pressure quickly, and their efforts to avoid pressure by other means soon fade. Some, however, are so distracted by pressure that progress stops. Their focus on what the trainer is doing to them prevents them from making the connection between the dummy in the mouth and the relief of pressure. Some dogs retreat into their boxes or act aggressively when we come to get them for their training session.

Fortunately, there are several means of applying pressure. We use the ear pinch or toe hitch, and occasionally the e-collar in the continuous mode (usually at a low setting). Those dogs that are distracted by one form of pressure will sometimes tolerate another. Some react negatively to the ear pinch. We have found that taking hold of the collar can badly distract dogs, whereas holding a lead attached to the collar usually does not. Holding the collar while applying the ear pinch may be too distracting for some.

We have switched individuals from ear pinch to toe hitch with good results. The toe hitch requires putting dogs on a table, usually with restraints. We have also switched dogs from toe hitch to e-collar with good results. That is, the dogs have seemed to better grasp "turning off pressure," and showed less resistance at the beginning of training sessions.

We are not confident the e-collar is the best for most dogs. Some dogs seem more distracted by collar pressure than by other means. We usually try the toe hitch or ear pinch first, then try the e-collar if the dog responds poorly to the others. The details of the toe hitch procedure are given at the end of this chapter.

Unstable response

Some retrievers respond to force-fetching with an aggressive lunge for the dummy. This is okay if the dog is calm but positive, but not so good if he is agitated. If the dog grabs the dummy fast but spits it out, mouths it compulsively and/or drops it, seemingly unable to concentrate and hold on, he may be emotionally worked up. Dogs in this state do not learn as well as those on a more even keel, and are prone to developing mouth problems. It is important to correct this response when you see it, instead of trying to build advanced training on a weak foundation.

A nervous response to force-fetching may be an indication of a dog that is excitable in general, and will benefit from deliberate handling as discussed in the chapters on Mouth Problems and Line Manners. It can also be a sign that too much pressure has been applied. Calm, methodical, low-pressure review of holding and fetching will help in either case. Watch for mouthing and dropping of dummies to reappear as training advances, and don't push ahead too fast.

Refusals

By "refusals," we mean instances when pressure is applied and the dog makes no move to reach for the dummy. We are convinced that many of these are the result of advancing too fast. No matter how obvious you think you have made your training, simplifying it even more is almost always a good solution to refusals. In dog training, success begets success. Failure tends to lead to more failure. Perhaps a dog loses confidence he can stop the pressure, even though he did so in the past. Keeping sessions short and limiting demands so as to maintain a high success rate gets faster results than trying to jump ahead. Try not to see these adjustments as giving in to a contrary animal, but as controlling his learning by controlling what you ask him to do.

Outside of the Big Three retriever breeds, we have encountered individuals that were extremely difficult to force fetch, including some we could not get retrieving.

Dog won't retrieve following force-fetching

Many retrievers quit retrieving during force-fetching, but start again after the process is complete. For most others, the walking fetch drill convinces them to pick up and deliver any dummy they see. Gradually increasing the length of tosses will get them retrieving willingly. A few dogs are more reluctant. After all of the formal work on fetching, a retrieve seems out of the question. These dogs must be started retrieving again somehow, before their training can continue.

Different solutions work on different dogs. Try a low-pressure approach first, as described for puppies that quit retrieving, in the Puppy Issues chapter. Be willing to relax obedience demands in the process. Once the dog is retrieving, it's usually easy to clean up the retrieve and get perfect deliveries.

If you can't get a retrieve by informal methods, establish a pile at close range. First, introduce the stick and get your retriever fetching in response to stick pressure. Follow this with a "walking fetch" drill, where dummies are lying on the ground several feet apart and you heel your dog up and have him fetch each, using stick pressure on some of the fetches. This establishes picking up dummies he did not just see you drop. Next start the dog fetching from a "pile" of two dummies, about one step away. Toss both down, have him fetch one and then the other, and repeat. Add pressure with the stick. Move back half a step and repeat. In subsequent sessions move farther away, keeping the pile at the same location. This goes much more slowly than with a dog that is eagerly retrieving, and it is difficult to get the dog to go unless the pile is in sight. In short cover, you will probably be able to get your dog going the distance of a short hand throw. Next you can try hand throws near the location of the pile, then gradually farther away. Work at this easy distance for a time and wait for the dog's enthusiasm to return.

With dogs that still don't retrieve, we have resorted to forcing the dog all the way to the dummy with the e-collar. We set the collar on continuous at a low level, holding the button down from the time we say "fetch" until the dog gets the dummy. We start at short distances, and lengthen the distance at a pace that maintains success.

The Toe Hitch Method

The toe hitch is easiest to apply while dogs are restrained on a table. Attach a cord to the dog's foreleg above the wrist, then put a loop around the two middle toes so that when you pull the cord, the toes are squeezed together. Pressure is applied in a pattern similar to the ear pinch.

Some things may be done differently when using the toe hitch. It is feasible to omit the teaching of "Hold" and go directly to "Fetch." A few dogs are unduly distressed by work on "Hold," even when it is done only with verbal praise and correction. Others will not tolerate touching their muzzles. Pinching the ear will cause some dogs to clamp their mouths shut. Most will open their mouths when their toes are squeezed, giving the trainer an opportunity to slip the dummy

The cord is attached with a clove hitch above the joint, and a loop around the two middle toes.

The Lab reaches for the dummy when we pull on the cord.

in, establishing a connection between the dummy in the mouth and relief from pressure.

After reaching for the dummy is established, holding can be taught by re-applying the pressure immediately when the dog drops a dummy. Following this, use toe pressure to proceed through the stages to picking dummies up from the table.

Because it is inconvenient to apply the toe hitch to a dog on the ground, we complete the procedure by conditioning to the ear pinch in place of the toe hitch. We start by applying the ear pinch and requiring a reach of only three or four inches. Usually within one session we can work all the way through to fetches from the table.

Some dogs will bite the first time their ear is pinched. Keep the pressure on, but not excessive. Make it clear that fetching will make it stop. Usually, attempts to bite stop quickly.

Once fetching from the table without pressure is established, a few sessions' practice on the ground will usually suffice. If the change inspires resistance, try using two checkcords as described above.

REAL
DOGS

BENTLEY

by Amy

WHEN A DOG DOES NOT respond well to pressure, or lacks motivation to retrieve, we have little leverage over his behavior. If the dog is to be trained, creativity may be needed.

Bentley is a show-bred golden retriever. When he arrived for training, it appeared that there was little chance of success through pressure or creating excitement for retrieving. He had responded poorly to force in prior obedience training, and had no working retrievers close-up in his pedigree. Fortunately, Bentley's owner did not have rigid expectations. On the contrary, her goal was simply to realize Bentley's retrieving potential, however much or little it might be.

Bentley's owner thought non-force training would benefit her dog, and approved our using mainly positive methods. I had been practicing "reinforcement" techniques on my own puppies. Bentley is very bright and attached to the idea of having things his own way. His interest in finding ways to make things happen turned out to be the handle I needed to get him working. It wasn't easy at first. I had learned to get dogs to do simple things using rewards, but Bentley was more interested in trying to outmaneuver me than in learning tricks. How could I correct Bentley's misbehavior without my stick, choke or pinch collar, and e-collar?

I discussed Bentley with a friend, behavior modification and aggression specialist Sue Alexander. She taught me some non-force techniques for controlling unwanted behavior. The most powerful, as I recall, was "play my way or I won't play." When Bentley acted up, or refused to try what I wanted him to, I hooked his checkcord to a tree and got out another dog. It worked.

Bentley learned his obedience and got nearly through force-fetch using verbal praise and admonishment. Good timing and Bentley's aptitude for this kind of training made it work; I think the mechanics of handling food would have made things more awkward. I completed force-fetching with the aid of momentary nicks with the e-collar. Bentley tolerated these, and made a breakthrough to reliable fetching.

In the field, we kept Bentley's retrieves short so as not to exceed his ambition. He was a precise marker, and became more enthusiastic. I undertook teaching him to line and cast. I shortened our single-T yard pattern to half its usual length. He soon learned to line and cast, even accepting pressure to go in the form of a stick to the hindquarters. Bentley's owner had modified her instructions to allow us to use our judgment regarding force. His training was progressing so well that we doubted switching to a traditional program would be an improvement. We have always found some form of forcing on "Back" essential, however, hence the stick. We subscribe to short training sessions, particularly in yard basics. Bentley's yard sessions were shortened even more.

Next I taught Bentley to do a blind retrieve in the field. Bentley was, by this time, looking pretty peppy on his single and double marks, but blinds seemed to drain his motivation. He became sluggish on marks as well as blinds, and started giving no-goes. We were already rewarding his efforts, making blinds easy so he could get them in one or two casts. If we had a dog that was eager on marks but disliked blinds, we might concentrate entirely on blinds until he developed enthusiasm for them. Bentley's case was different. His lack of motivation on blinds was affecting all of his work. We reduced his blinds, running only two a week and keeping them short. It was a good call; Bentley's pep on marks returned, and he made progress on blinds, learning to handle adequately out to 75 yards.

In due course Bentley's owner picked him up. Our responsibility now was to help her make the most of his training. Our experience is that force in training aids in the transfer from one handler to another, but Bentley had had little. Moreover, while we often refer owners to obedience trainers and retriever clubs in their vicinity, Bentley's training was so unconventional we thought it unlikely his owner would find someone who could provide much help. Traditionally-minded retriever owners rely on forceful solutions to most problems. Reinforcement-oriented trainers tend to use food. Fortunately, Bentley retrieved well for his owner, and she readily caught on to the essentials of motivating her dog. With the aid of emails and

occasional long-distance conversations with us, Bentley's owner has continued his training.

Bentley's progress has been interesting. Around a year ago, he started breaking and misbehaving on line. The picture his owner painted was of a dog out-of-control with eagerness to retrieve. Bentley had been running hunt tests but could not pass unless he was steady. We explained how to address the problem with his manners—don't walk him to the line unless he controls himself, don't let him retrieve unless he is both calm and steady, and honor only when necessary. Bentley's owner got his line manners under control and earned a number of hunt test passes.

With all of the special treatment and innovative solutions

he has required, Bentley has come a long way. Thus far, he does not seem to have reached the limits of his potential. Bentley's owner, sensitive to her dog's idiosyncrasies and quick to grasp and apply training ideas, is ideally suited to bringing out his talents. We are watching with interest to see what Bentley and his owner may accomplish.

CHAPTER 15

MANNERS

D OGS THAT PERFORM well in the field may have bad manners elsewhere. The most responsive trainees can be the worst offenders—full of motivation and the desire for approval, they pester their owners, and others, when not working.

Individual owners' definitions of bad manners vary. A few things, such as jumping up on people and weaving between people's legs, are potentially dangerous as well as unpleasant. Others, such as begging and demanding attention, are acceptable to some owners. What's important is your choice. The point is that you can choose—you can teach your retriever to behave as you wish.

Improving manners generally means getting your dog to stop doing what you do not like. If the dog does something repeatedly, he has learned to do it. If the factors that taught him are still present, they will work against your efforts to make him stop. If you can identify and remove the motivation, you can usually get rid of the problem behavior. Usually behavior has been rewarded by you or a family member, or by something in the environment. Consistency is the key. Just as a good retriever is persistent in his hunt for a bird, despite several failures, he will continue his bad manners even if rewarded only occasionally. If you can eliminate the reward and apply sufficient discouragement, his behavior will change as soon as he recognizes the absence of the reward. Habits established by infrequent rewards take the longest to eradicate.

Attention is the reward that instigates most bad manners. Dogs are ignored when calm and quiet, and get attention when they misbehave. Punishment such as yelling or throwing water on them may be taken as a reward. Food is sometimes the culprit, particularly in the case of begging. Being let in the house after scratching at the door is certainly rewarding. Some behavior is inherently rewarding. Chewing, digging, and in some cases, barking, either feel good or relieve stress and boredom, or both. You can't take the reward away, so we recommend managing the dog to limit damage. Confinement in a crate or run prevents damage to furnishings and yard. Concrete or pavers prevent digging. We have found bark collars to be effective, although they can only be used a few hours per day. Keeping the dog in the house usually prevents nuisance barking.

Once you have identified the reward, try to find a way to prevent it. It is natural to respond to a dog that, having been quiet, begins pestering you. It helps to make a habit of doling out brief attention, such as a calm "Good boy," or a pat or a treat, from time to time when he is behaving well. A good tactic is to teach him to "Go lie down," that is, go to the other side of the room, lie down, and stay there. Then, when he pesters you, tell him to go lie down. Be consistent! If you respond by petting him one time in ten, or one time in twenty, the hope for that reward will perpetuate the behavior.

If going between your legs is a problem, teach yourself to keep your feet together, and never pet your prospective gun dog when he is between your legs. Outdoors, give him a smack with your training stick if he tries it. Get your family to cooperate on this one, at least to the extent of not rewarding the behavior. Dogs can learn what works with each member of the family. You can teach him to leave you alone, but it is vital that he not knock down strangers or hunting partners. He needs to understand that ducking between people's legs is never allowed.

Retrievers seem to learn to jump up on people even when their owners are careful never to reward them for it. They jump on each other while playing, and don't get obvious rewards from the other dog's response. We could say that they are programmed to find the act of jumping inherently rewarding. Jumping up can be effectively discouraged, though. If we anticipate the jump and step back quickly with an expression of dismay, the dog's paws do not connect and the jump fails as a social overture. Most of our new trainees stop jumping after one or two tries. It might take longer for a person who has previously allowed the behavior to get the same response. Some

Retrievers have a strong tendency to jump up.

retrievers, particularly Labradors, are less sensitive and don't get the message quickly. They may need an attention-getter before they notice we are not rewarding their jumping. We take a metal feeding pan, similar in weight to an aluminum pie pan, hold it at shoulder height, and strike the dog over the muzzle or head as he is on his way up. This works quickly without injuring them.

As with other manners problems, retrievers are capable of learning that they won't get anywhere jumping on you, but they will with others. To achieve good manners towards all, you may need to get the cooperation of your family, and even arrange to have some "visitors," instructed in advance by you, come to the house and support your lessons. If you enlist helpers, we recommend that you go farther and obtain their help in teaching your retriever that he only gets attention from strangers when he is sitting calmly.

We teach our dogs to sit still while being petted. Praise constitutes less of a distraction if the trainee remains calm. It also makes him more pleasant to be around.

When raising a puppy, pet him only when all four feet are on the ground, then work toward the requirement to sit. With active older dogs, it may be a little harder to get started. Dogs learn to maintain their composure through practice, not by correction, so we require short periods of calmness at first, then increase. If touching a dog makes him jumpy, we begin by hav-

A touch on the back of the neck is minimally disruptive.

ing him "Sit" (and "Stay" if so taught), and touch him lightly on the neck with the training stick, and praise calmly if he is still. Work up to extended touching, stroking him with the stick on different parts of his body. Next, introduce stroking with your hand, beginning with a brief touch to the neck. Once he tolerates your touch without coming unglued, practice petting him every day, requiring that he sits and remains still. If he rises, turns his head, or makes any quick moves, remove your hands. Once he makes the connection that jumpiness stops the attention, he'll apply himself. After this has been established, enlist helpers and repeat the process extending good manners to all.

A dangerous form of misbehavior occurs when a retriever bumps into a person's legs. A muscular, fast-moving retriever can hit hard, potentially causing serious injury. Retrievers are capable, however, of learning to be aware of people and avoiding accidental contact, even when playing with other dogs. Our response to this is crude. We simply yell and act as angry as we can, for perhaps five or ten seconds. Most dogs get the message and avoid further collisions.

We also work to teach dogs not to body-slam each other. Usually we let only one new member out in a well-behaved group. We try to have a stick ready, but whether we do or not, we make sure we get the dog's attention, interrupt its play, and make our anger known loudly enough so that it knows something is wrong. We have known dogs to suffer career-ending injuries in collisions, so preventing them is a priority.

Pulling on a leash is, like other forms of bad manners, learned. Like jumping up, the tendency to learn pulling is strong. Dogs innately resist a steady pull (or a steady push). If we try to use a leash to pull a dog around, or just let the leash tighten on walks, that innate response quickly becomes a habit.

Dogs that come in for training un-learn the pulling habit at different rates. Some get it in a couple of days, with little effort on our part. Others have taken over a month to learn.

The first step in breaking the pulling habit is for you to stop pulling on the leash. Try switching to a lead fifteen or twenty feet long, and hold it only by the handle. Yes, it's going to drag on the ground and get looped around your dog's feet. Let it. Most retrievers will stay closer than twenty feet. When yours gets to the end of the lead, make sure the tightening of the lead is brief. If your dog responds to the pressure of the lead with a tug, jerk hard enough so as to suddenly get him back into the zone where it is slack.

If your dog doesn't stop trying to pull on the long lead, introduce correction. You can fit him with a pinch collar, and give a hard jerk on that, or even turn and get some momentum in the other direction before he gets to the end of the lead. You can use an e-collar on momentary mode to give your dog a nick just as he tightens the lead (then jerk him back to create slack). You can call him and require him to come and sit by you any time he starts to pull. Individual dogs respond better to different measures, so if at first yours does not improve, experiment.

Tightening of the lead must be kept brief.

Most retrievers readily learn to walk on a loose lead.

When your retriever clearly avoids tightening the long lead, switch to a shorter lead and repeat the corrections as necessary. From then on, remember not to pull, and the lesson should stick. Don't allow anyone else to walk your dog while you are retraining him. After good leash manners are established, teach anyone else who walks him how to maintain them. We have found that proper walking on lead transfers well from us to others, as long as they learn not to pull on the dog.

For manners issues not covered here, we advise that you try to correct the situation that encourages the misbehavior, and then target the problem behavior itself. There is one annoying manners issue we have been unable to correct. We have owned two bitches, a golden retriever and a German shepherd, who were prone to mouth our hands. With both, we found that regardless of whether we tried punishment or withholding attention, we could stop the behavior but the bitch would act depressed. In most cases, we feel bad manners are accidental and the dog would be just as happy behaving differently, but these two bitches seemed to have a need to mouth our hands. Much as we dislike dogs mouthing us, in the end we allowed it because the bitches' dispirited behavior was worse. It's possible, of course, that they conned us.

DANGEROUS BEN

by John

THE SUBJECT OF MANNERS brings to mind how hazardous the actions of an unruly dog in the duck blind or boat can be. The subject of this story is a yellow Lab I bought when I lived in Maine.

I read a Lab-for-sale ad in the local newspaper. I needed a retriever to replace my Lab who had recently died. When I arrived at the seller's house I saw a good-looking, husky yellow Lab chained to his box in the back yard. When I got out to look at him, the lady of the house appeared. I asked if this was the dog that was for sale, and she said, "Yes."

I followed this inquiry with some questions concerning his breeding, of which she knew nothing, and any training he had been given, which was nil. When I asked the price she said $50. Even 35 years ago, the price was attractive, and Ben was bold, active, and good looking.

I took him home, did some preliminary obedience, threw him a couple of dummies and dead pigeons, and took him hunting on a tidal marsh the following weekend. During the course of the morning, I crippled a goldeneye. The duck was a strong swimmer and my efforts to get Ben to make the retrieve were unsuccessful. I proceeded to chase the injured duck with my boat intending, when I got close, to cut off the motor, wait for the duck to surface, and finish him off with a shot on the water. This plan was thwarted by Ben wildly jumping around in the boat in front of me as I tried to shoot the duck. After a few efforts in which the boat was so destabilized I couldn't get off an accurate shot, I whacked Ben across the back with the barrels of my shotgun about midway between the muzzles and the action.

The resulting jar to the mechanism of the gun discharged both barrels into the bottom of the boat. We were in 10-12' of cold salt water. My immediate reaction was that I'd never make it to shore in a swamped boat before I was overcome by hypothermia. I was astounded to see, though, that no water came into the boat.

I had stacked several bags of decoys in the front half of the boat, and the shot columns had made a direct hit on two of them. That, and a heavy quilted gun case lying on top of the decoy bags, had been sufficient to stop the shot from blowing a hole in the bottom of the boat.

Shaken by the close call, I headed for shore. When I reached the landing I pulled the boat up to examine the damage, but could find nothing beyond a dozen shattered decoys and a gun case with a gaping hole. I looked everywhere for the shot pellets, but didn't find any. That, perhaps, was the strangest aspect of the whole incident. Enough to make one superstitious.

I learned two lessons from this potentially fatal mishap. One, never assume that a gun with the safety on is free from the possibility of accidental discharge. In many guns, the trigger seers are perilously close to releasing the hammers, and a good jolt may be all it takes to drop them on the firing pins.

The other is to ensure that all retrievers hunted from a boat or blind are calm, quiet, and steady. If not, they are more of a liability than an asset. When taking young or inexperienced retrievers hunting under such conditions, we recommend confining your efforts to controlling your dog. Let your partner do the shooting.

INDEX

ABOUT THE AUTHORS

John and Amy Dahl have over 40 years of retriever training experience between them. They have won numerous field-trials, five State Gun Dog Championships, handled six dogs to Field Championships, and trained owner-handled dogs to their titles, including two Chesapeakes and two Dual Champions. They are popular columnists for The Retriever Journal and Just Labs magazines, and they are the authors of the book, The 10-Minute Retriever, published by Willow Creek Press.